Life Between Here and There

SAMUEL KWARTENG

&

DONALD MACLAREN

DEDICATION

To my parents who helped to give me new dreams; to my children who have their dreams to fulfill; and to students everywhere who should get their education and fulfill their greater dreams.

CONTENTS

ACKNOWLEDGMENTS

I would like to thank all those who are dear to me: my Lord and Savior Jesus Christ; Donald MacLaren in preparation of this inspirational book; my Mom and Dad; my brothers and sisters; friends and family; my children whom I love dearly—my precious daughter Hannah, my handsome boys, Gabriel, Shadrach, and Gideon; Maybell for giving birth to my lovely children; the United States Postal Service; the National Association of Letter Carriers (NALC) and the credit union; my coworkers for their support and encouragement; and the Queens Ghana Seventh Day Adventist Church, First Ghana Seventh Day Adventist Church, North Bronx Ghana Seventh Day Adventist Church, Yonkers Ghana Seventh Day Adventist Church, Brooklyn Ghana Seventh Day Adventist Church, Long Island Ghana Seventh Day Adventist Church, and all the Christians around the world. Hold onto your faith. Never lose hope in God. There is a God.

INTRODUCTION

My Dream

Wisdom for today: The purpose of life is to find better opportunities.

At age seven, I told my mother, "I had a dream last night. I saw myself working in the post office."

It was not a big dream such as becoming a doctor, lawyer, singer or a scientist. Children at a certain age start thinking about their future. Parents and other adults will start asking children what they think they may want to do in life. Questions about the future help the child to reach out to explore and begin to connect to the future.

I took my dream as a revelation. The post office job was what I was supposed to do. It was part of a plan that God had for me. Most people would laugh at that goal and say, "Maybe you should try for another job that is more important," or "Are you sure that is all God wants you to do?" They are good challenging questions to my 'dream' job, but I felt confident that I should pursue this job as my priority.

1

Unfortunately, I lived in a country that had educational limitations—no computers, no government support, no student grants; and many students dropped out for financial reasons. No one in the family spoke of going to college. Just graduating from high school could be an impossible dream for many reasons.

Whether my mother believed that my dream would come true, I had no way of knowing at my young age of seven. I had no awareness of the difficulties that lay ahead of me to achieve the post office job or any job at all.

As I grew older, I had other dreams, and I continued to believe God had sent me messages even as a child that actually came to fruition: coming to the United States, having a wife and children, and writing a book to inspire others.

My parents taught me and my siblings to go to church. As a child, I learned to pray and to have faith that God answers prayers. As I grew older, I learned that dreams and prayers do not get answered right away. God works in His own ways in His own timing. In some cases, some dreams and prayers may not get answered the way we wanted them to turn out. Does that mean that we should lose faith in God?

When what we dream and pray for doesn't come, that's when we learn about patience. For that reason, I've learned a lot about patience over the years, and I'm still learning. In addition, I have learned that some dreams may come, but interference by others may interfere with or destroy our dreams. All I can say is that God always has lessons for us to learn. After all, none of us knows our future perfectly.

In the end, all of us can be humbled because God teaches us that life does not guarantee an easy journey to our accomplishments. New surprises, changes, and challenges will thwart us on the journey. God may seem to stop us or redirect us when we are otherwise happy just to keep going along our set path. The devil and those who are evil are always around us and evil influences can change our future. Jesus had difficult times with the devil and those who set out to hurt him, so I, too, cannot always assume my life as a Christian will be easy.

Things happen for good, although some things seem to bring bad results. One never knows just how God works. He always has new doors to open for us.

But going back to age seven, my first important dream was to work in the post office. It seemed a rather small dream, but to my seven year old brain, it was something I felt that I could accomplish. However, I had no idea of my mother's thoughts when I revealed my dream. If I had been able to hear her doubting me, I would have asked her why. In the years ahead, I would learn what she was thinking: even little goals may not be possible, because you're growing up in Africa.

Photo credit: Rita Gyamfuah
Figure 1 Sample home of the wealthy in Ghana.

Photo credit: Rita Gyamfuah
Figure 2   Sample home of the poor in Ghana.

CHAPTER 1

PRIOR TO MY BIRTH

Wisdom for today: The best countries are the ones who cultivate their citizens.

In 1976, I had a normal birth at home which at the time involved a midwife coming to my parents' home to help deliver me. I had been born into a country that once had the distinction of being called the Gold Coast. The country's name kept changing, depending on which European country had colonized it: Portuguese Gold Coast in the 15th century; the Dutch Gold Coast; the Swedish Gold Coast; the Danish Gold Coast; the German Gold Coast; and the British Gold Coast. The country's name still retained the name "gold" in it through the centuries because of the availability of this precious resource. I am surprised that Spain never sent a fleet of ships during the time of the Conquistadors to steal my country's gold, but apparently Spain selfishly preferred to focus its strategic sights on scouring the New World for the gold purportedly hidden in South and Central America.

Meanwhile, whatever gold and wealth the Europeans

managed to mine and steal from my country was never properly shared with the people there. Through the centuries, my country still holds a position as one of the top gold and diamond mining countries in the world. As I grew up in my country, I came to realize that the country's citizens always had one age-old question: who was enjoying the wealth of the gold and diamond mining? From the poverty of the country, all the wealth amassed by other countries was not trickling down to provide needed services to the people.

After World War II, the world's countries were changing. There were new borders, new countries, and new country names. A push for self-government had actually begun in the 1940s to allow my country to break away from colonization and become independent. It took until March, 1957, for the glorious day of independence from Britain to become official. Britain allowed the Gold Coast to become a self-governed country with a constitutional government. My country's new leaders chose a new name: The Republic of Ghana. Ghana was a native word that meant "warrior kings." Ghana led other African countries by becoming the first African country to break away from colonization. Also, the new government designed a new flag using three symbolic colors: red for the blood shed for the country's independence; gold for the country's natural wealth; green for the rich grasslands; and a black star in the middle for the African people's emancipation.

My country's freedom had come 19 years before my birth. Despite being one country, I was born into a country with over 79 languages based on the major tribes: Asante, Nzema, Ewe, Fante, Boron, Dajomba, Dangme, Dagaba, Akyem, Ga, and Akuapem. However, the British colonization helped to establish English as the recognized official language. While growing up, I spoke my native Asante at home and learned English in the missionary church schools.

I would be taught that Ghana had great natural resources including gold, timber, diamonds, bauxite, and manganese. It was also one of the world's top producers of gold, petroleum, and natural gas. As for agricultural products, Ghana had established itself as a leader in cocoa, ranking as the number two cocoa producer in the world. It can be noted that cocoa refers to the tropical evergreen tree that produces seeds which are ground into a powder known as cocoa used to make chocolate. Ghana's other resources are rubber, coconuts, coffee, pineapples, cashews, and pepper. Also, I learned that Ghana had the largest artificial lake in the world—Lake Volta.

Although Ghana seemed to be successful, I began wondering as I grew older about a lot of things: Would I ever be part of Ghana's wealth? Would the government see its citizens as its greatest wealth? Would this independent government lead the way in helping the citizens get an excellent education and turning Ghana into the number one African country? Was I doomed to a life of extreme poverty that I saw around me? Why didn't the government realize that the poverty of the citizens only keeps the country poor? Could I escape Ghana's poverty or was I predestined to live and die in poverty?

Photo credit: Rita Gyamfuah
Figure 3   Ashanti traditional home.

Photo credit: Rita Gyamfuah
Figure 4   Ashanti traditional home.

CHAPTER 2

LIFE BEGINS

Wisdom for today: As I grew up listening to the church's teachings and my father's Christian guidance, I learned that I had to recognize and stay away from trouble, because trouble is always next to us and waiting to bring us problems.

I was born in Kumasi, the capital of the Ashanti region of Ghana. My mother delivered me at home with the help of a midwife, which was the common practice at the time. Hospitals and doctors were rare and people didn't have insurance or money to pay for the medical costs. God blessed me and kept me alive through the delivery.

At home, I first learned to speak Twi, the language of my Asante tribe.

I can say that my father was a good man. In fact, he helped provide a stable home for us. His education was not extensive, but his family had paid for him to go to an agriculture school in Ghana. His mother had made financial sacrifices in order to help him. It can be said that her money was well spent because he turned out to be a good son, husband, and father.

After his graduation, he worked for the government as a consultant to farmers, helping them to choose what to plant and how to raise better crops. His job required daily traveling to the local and some remote villages. Although he had a government job and even an important job in helping the farmers, the government did not provide a car. He was forced to rely on three forms of transportation: walking, public transportation, and a bicycle. During Ghana's rainy season, it meant he had to walk around in wet clothes until he could get back home to change. On the other hand, summers meant droughts, and hot weather that climbed to over 100 degrees, and a muggy, tropical humidity that soaked everyone's clothes as they walked around outside. Air conditioning was only available for the wealthy and businesses.

The government paid him enough that he could afford his own apartment. That was a blessing since our grandparents and other relatives lived in mud huts with leaf roofs. When it rained, water dripped in.

Father advised farmers who were mostly growing cocoa, coffee, and oranges. He taught them how to use fertilizers and pesticides that came mostly from Europe. In addition to teaching the farmers, he supervised 10 to 15 workers so they could go to other villages to teach the farmers how to farm better. He also had to go back to the villages every six months to check on the farmers whom he had taught to see if they were doing better and needed more assistance. He played a very important role in helping the country achieve better farming results for the farmers which prevented famines. As for the farmers, they appreciated the government sending my father because they had no money to pay for his training and they lived hand to mouth by what they managed to sell every day at the markets.

As for paying taxes, the government tax collectors went around the markets and collected a tax for using the stall at the market for that day. If a farmer could not make it to the market, no one would come by to ask the farmer to pay a tax. Did the tax collectors keep some of the money from the government? It's a good question. I don't know if the government really knew how much was collected every day at the markets. If receipts were given, I would hope they were an honest accounting of the tax money.

Besides his important role of helping the farmers and subsequently the government, father was also a church elder in the local Seventh Day Adventist Church. The Adventists had established some churches and schools in the area that were well attended. The main difference between the Adventists and other Christians is that the Adventists teach that God wants us to worship Him on the Sabbath, which would mean Saturdays. All the other Christian denominations worshiped on Sundays as a reminder of Jesus Christ's resurrection on the third day. I came to see that our parents believed in a good Christian home. The teachings that I learned in the church and at home were guiding me through the difficult times of my life. Father, being a great Christian believer, never gave us a chance to do unnecessary things like drugs.

By the time I reached fifteen, my parents realized that Ghana could not provide a better life for them or for us. They had to leave. It was a difficult decision, but millions of families have made the decision to leave a country and go to another country. There is a long history of boatloads of people leaving their countries in search of new opportunities: the Pilgrims sailed away from England in search of religious freedom; Cubans in the last century staked their lives on flimsy small boats to escape communism and the Fidel Castro; and lately hundreds of thousands of people have paid exorbitant fees to traffickers to crowd them on boats from Libya, Tunisia, and Turkey to bet their lives on reaching Europe to start new lives and find new opportunities.

Once our parents left, my siblings and I didn't have them around to push us to go to church. If we wanted to go, we went. By fifteen, I had become used to the support and encouragement of the church, so I continued going every Saturday. My parents had trained us well to respect our opportunities and not to let others lead us down the wrong path. I had to realize that trouble was always around me if I let it get the best of me. I could destroy my life at an early age, but I had been trained to avoid trouble, because trouble was never worth what problems and heartaches it brought.

Photo credit: Emmanuel Taah

Figure 5   Mother carrying baby and yam.

CHAPTER 3

EVERYONE HELPED

Wisdom today: Happiness can come from the helpful support of everyone around us.

I'm glad to say that father and mother never had any problems. That means that they didn't fight, argue, hit each other, or get drunk in front of us. Whatever financial problems or other problems that had to do with surviving, they worked together to solve.

Since father was allowed to hire other workers, he hired mother to be an agriculture consultant. Mother did finish high school and went on to vocational school. She never made it to college, but father and mother were happy to work and travel to the villages together.

Besides consulting with farmers, father and mother had their own small farm and a small garden next to the house. My maternal grandparents lived on a small farm and my parents would go to their farm to help on their days off. When they could not make it to the farm, they would pay some people to help weed around the farm.

Dad and mom both had the heavy chore of carrying water home. Dad could not use his bicycle to carry the water, because the water would be too heavy to balance on the bicycle and in the rainy season the dirt roads turned to mud.

Once a week, mother would go to the market to make some money. She would either resell fruits and vegetables she bought from other farmers or sell produce they grew on our family farm.

In Ghana, we had no babysitters to watch over us. Children played outside and were on their own without adult supervision. Parents would teach their children that they were okay outside as long as they did not go into the bush by themselves. Children were watched and generally supervised by any family members and neighbors who were around. In fact, people permitted any adult to discipline a child. It was certainly an open society for discipline, but it spared the families from paying for babysitters.

In Ghana, children were taught that they have to obey adults, even if they disagree with the adults. Children were not allowed to talk back when an adult is speaking. My parents did a good job of training me to obey them, my grandmother, my uncle, and all adults. That made life easier for the adults and avoided unnecessary confrontations with children. The first social lesson that children learn in Ghana is to respect adults and that they have no authority over adults.

Photo credit: Rita Gyamfuah
Figure 6   Wood carver.

CHAPTER 4

MOTHER'S IMPORTANT ROLE

Wisdom today: The bible teaches that finding a good woman is like finding a treasure and I believe that. Not only did my father find a good treasure in his wife, but I found a good treasure in my mother.

When Mom went to the market, she would buy fish. Since we lived too far from the ocean to eat ocean fish, the fish came from the many local rivers, caught by fishermen baiting a hook. As a child, I learned to fish with a hook and, sometimes, we would kill birds for food too.

At the time, both maternal and paternal grandparents were alive, but I mostly went to my maternal grandparents because they were closer. My paternal grandparents belonged to another tribe and lived in a village farther away.

Although Mom and Dad came from two different tribes, Dad had gone to school in Asenfosu, a town where my mom and her parents lived and where she attended high school. After graduating from agriculture school, they met in her town. Dad ultimately was able to show that he could afford to take care of a wife, a requirement for marriage in Ghana. He proposed and they got married.

Every town and village has its own market day. Our market day was Tuesday.

The growing season was during the rainy season between February and April. In summer, there was no rain so the people would irrigate using water from the rivers or a well.

Mom and her mother as well as the local farmers would start Sundays and Mondays to arrange their produce to the market on the roadside after making the trek with the produce piled on their heads. It was always a balancing act and people could only make money according to how much they could get to the market. Imagine American companies trying to make money by how much products their employees could carry to a market. Those lucky enough to have a popular item would pay others to carry the produce for them, but paying others to help was an infrequent luxury.

To get ready for market day, every family had someone to carry their produce to a selected site along the road. On the market day, a van would stop to pick up the produce. Farmers would leave their produce sitting at the pickup site for as many as three days. Since the whole village was involved in getting the produce to market, no one stole. People simply used different colors to identify their produce. Mom used the color blue, while another farmer would use red and so on.

On Tuesday mornings around 6 a.m., mom would be on her way to the market to set up her produce table. She mostly bought and sold plantains and cassava all year, but my parents also grew and sold cocoa, yams, tomatoes, carrots, cabbage, lettuce, and corn.

Since Mom traveled around with Dad helping the farmers, she knew people from the villages. She was a successful seller and ended up selling everything which meant that she brought money home and never returned with unsold produce. When we were babies and young toddlers, mom was strong enough to carry one of us on her back as she walked with the produce on her head.

Any children left at home and who did not go to the market with their mothers always had lots of relatives—sometimes, brothers, uncles, aunts, sisters—living in the same house or nearby so someone would watch the kids until they were old enough to go to school. It was never considered wrong, immoral, or neglectful to leave a child in the home because family or neighbors would watch the children. Watching children represented a collective community babysitting service.

Photo credit: Emmanuel Taah
Figure 7   Sample market for the poor.

CHAPTER 5

Ghanaian Villages

Wisdom today: We have to respect the poorest people because they manage to take care of themselves and their children while enduring the worst of circumstances.

Living in a village in the bush represents the barest living standards. Some Ghanaians have lived in tents when they could not afford a house made of mud mortar.

Villagers with health problems have risked or succumbed to death because they could not count on ambulances to take them to a doctor or a hospital. The only option villagers for most villagers is to get to the nearest road with van service that could drive them to a city hospital quickly. There are no accurate records to know how many have died for lack of transportation to a medical facility, but the deaths must number in the thousands. Villagers have to carry a sick person to the road and then flag down a passing van and hope it is not already filled up. Of course, any passing car would do, but most people travel in vans. Vans have been the major form of transportation. It was common to see vans filled with people who would keep get out or on while the vans stop. Since the government has never been willing to provide a bus service, people have to rely on the private vans. This situation is in sharp contrast to the public transportation system in New York City.

In the cities, ambulances might be available occasionally, but they can be undependable if they are not close to someone's home or if they get stuck in traffic. Of course, those who are wealthy had better access to ambulances or to private cars to transport them to a medical facility in an emergency.

As an example, my maternal grandparents' village was about six miles from the road. If someone had to go to a hospital or clinic, the nearest town, Smithtown, was another six miles away for a total of about 12 miles to a medical facility. In fact, I lived with them at one time while in school and had to walk 12 miles one way to school and then after school, 12 miles back to their home. It was common for my friends and I to run, walk, and rest when we traveled greater distances on foot.

FAMILY PLANS FOR SCHOOL

In 1981, at age five, I embarked on my education in a public school for grades 1 to 6: The school—United Primary School—was operated by the Salvation Army and the Adventist church.

In Ghana, my education involved attending three schools. Fortunately, my parents made enough extra money from their farm that they could send me and my siblings off to school when we reached five.

The elementary school was far away, so I lived with my grandparents in their village which was closer to the school. Since my parents were not home all the time and dad had to stay overnight in some villages, my maternal grandparents took care of me. Their village area was in the Ashanti region of Ghana. The plan was I would live with them until I started junior high.

To prepare for the elementary school, I used to get up at 6 a.m. School went from 8 a.m. until 3:30 p.m. I started my school day by eating breakfast at my grandparents' hut. Most of the time, I missed lunch as did most of the other students because we had no money for lunch and the church school never provided a free-lunch program for the children. I usually arrived back at my grandparents' village around 6 p.m. We had dinner and then we would work on the farm. At night, we had no electricity. Kerosene lanterns became our source of light for studying or for walking around the bush at night. Everyone in our hut went to bed around 9 p.m. to be ready to start another day at 6 a.m. We lived life in the most basic ways and without any electronic entertainment that electricity would provide.

PUBLIC TRANSPORTATION PROBLEMS

Time spent with my grandparents taught me how more difficult their lives were than life in a small town where my parents lived. In my parents' town, there were vans. In the villages, there were no cars or even horses. People had to walk everywhere through the bush.

It was often difficult to get a van because the vans never had a set schedule. Often, night would come and I would still be waiting for a van in the dark. When I saw headlights, I waved the van to a stop in hopes of getting picked up. Sometimes, I was given a kerosene lamp to help me follow the path through the bush. There were nights I had to wait alone, but on other nights, there would be a few people there with me. At some places along the road, someone had cut a tree and made a crude bench out of a cut log where people could sit. When it rained, we got wet and had to endure standing in the rain. Snakes and scorpions lurked in the dark, but we had to take our chances. If people did not have kerosene lamps, they simply made a torch from a wood stick.

Without horses or donkeys at my grandparent's village, all of us had only one option—walk to the distant road. I can be thankful that they did not live 20 miles away from the road or I would be exhausted just trying to reach the road.

Photo credit: Rita Gyamfuah

Figure 8 People crowding onto a bus van. There used to be one train running north and south, but that has stopped. Public transportation does not exist to help the people.

CHAPTER 6

DANGERS IN THE BUSH

Wisdom today: Dangers lurk around us that can hurt or kill us if we are not vigilant about our surroundings.

I learned as a young boy about the dangers I had to watch out for as I walked through the bush. Snakes were always a common concern which could be close to my bare feet and bare legs.

Snakes are a problem in the bush. Needless to say, people have died after being bitten by one of Ghana's poisonous snakes. Snakes were known to lie on the road to warm themselves and bite anyone who didn't see them. I did get bitten by a poisonous snake when I was about eight or nine while working on the farm. My grandmother and some villagers rushed me to a local herbalist since clinics were further away and no one had a vehicle to take me to a doctor. The herbalist and local medicine man selected a special leaf and started rubbing it. The rubbing extracted some type of liquid that he put on my skin where I had been bitten. Somehow, the potion saved my life. I thank God that I was bitten only once in

Ghana despite at least 16 years of walking in the bush going back and forth to my grandparents and to school. After I felt better from the snake bite, I walked back to the road and waited for a van ride home. An adult went with me to make sure I would make it to the van.

Photo credit: Emmanuel Taah
Figure 9 Snakes can come into homes.

As a child, I was taught not to go into the bush alone or with my friends. The wild area around the village could certainly include wild animals, resulting in our being attacked, crippled, or killed. Where my grandparents lived, I occasionally saw the more dangerous animals of Africa that were known to attack humans—lions, panthers, African bush elephants, wild dogs, hippos, and spotted hyenas.

One large animal unique to Ghana is the Savannah monitor lizard which grows to between two to five feet. People actually hunt them because their skins can be exported for shoes and other products. The government has catered to the tourists who want to see the wild life and fauna by establishing 15 substantial national parks.

Another feature very popular with tourists, but not at all dangerous, are Ghana's 1,000 species of butterflies, whose numbers are larger than butterflies in North and South America combined. Sometimes I saw monkeys in the trees, and deer running past trees. Some people kept pigs at home as pets or raised them for food. Wild pigs had a bad reputation for digging up and eating dead bodies at the cemetery. In Ghana, I know that people ate pigs and squirrels and the popular food of lamb and goats.

Another favorite animal among those who could afford it were donkeys. As a Christian, I was reminded in the Bible that Jesus made His triumphal entrance into Jerusalem on a donkey. That seemed to be a strange, humble animal for the Messiah to ride. Donkeys are looked down on and considered a cheap work animal. They have none of the glamour of a stallion or the prancing horse. It is obvious that Jesus as the Messiah purposely did not enter Jerusalem on a white horse. The horse would have been the symbol of a military hero and the opposite message He had been proclaiming. This Jesus Messiah wanted to be a servant of all people and a donkey was an animal good enough animal to present himself as the Messiah, not as a military conqueror.

In my grandmother's village, I made friends with other

children and they showed me the two nearby rivers—one about two miles away and the other about five miles away. The rivers became the places where we learned to swim and take baths. However, the same water where we washed we brought back in buckets on our heads so our families could use the water at home for drinking and bathing. As a child, I didn't think much about whether the water was clean or polluted. Pollution would be possible from others taking baths, people washing their clothes, animal waste runoffs, or chemical runoffs from agriculture fertilizers. I never heard of anyone becoming sick from the water, but the rivers had running water that likely cleared the water and flushed any pollutants down river. Anyhow, I'm still alive.

Life with my grandparents was considered very primitive by western standards. Their home of mortar walls had a roof made of bamboo and palm tree leaves. There were only two rooms, one for visitors and one for us. It leaked when it rained hard, making us have to sit up until daylight came in the morning before we could go out and fix the roof. Their house had no electricity so we never had the luxury of air conditioning, ceiling fans, or electronic aids. We simply had to survive summer's exhausting heat and humidity the best we could.

My grandparents cooked on big stones, using old, dried branches for firewood. Since we had to get water from the river, that meant walking two miles to it, then walk back two miles, all the while balancing a water bucket on our head—a total of four miles just for a bucket of water.

The children in my grandparent's village were barefoot and occasionally a splinter of wood would go into their feet. I had shoes because my parents worked and could afford to buy one pair every few years. Walking through the bush was never fun. The bushes were often uncomfortably wet either from the morning dew or the rain, so wet clothes became the norm. We never had umbrellas or ponchos to protect us. That meant we simply endured having to walk around in wet clothes.

When there was a drought, life got harder. For one thing, people had to walk as much as 10 miles to find water because the rivers or wells had dried up. In fact, droughts are not that unusual because Ghana is located near the equator on the hottest part of the planet.

Photo credit: Emmanuel Taah
Figure 10   People cooling off.

Photo credit: Rita Gyamfuah
Figure 11   Bobiri Forest Butterfly.

Photo credit: Rita Gyamfuah
Figure 12   Kakum canopy walkway.

CHAPTER 7

PREPARING FOR SCHOOL IN GHANA

Wisdom today: If a country's government neglects its youth, that country becomes weaker.

School in Ghana is totally different from school in the U.S. and the developed countries. In America, the government helps with everything from lunch to grants, and some students only pay for supplies. The students and their families in Ghana are mostly on their own. In Ghana, students pay for everything, from lunch and the required school uniforms from fist grade until they finish their schooling. Many parents cannot afford to pay for the school fees, uniforms, supplies, and lunches. If the family does not have the money, their children do not go to school. Also, Ghana does not provide public school buses.

After elementary school, students go to grades seven to nine called J.S.S (Junior Secondary School). Again, education requires money without which poor children do not get educated. The lack of education among Ghanaian children is a national tragedy. In a country that makes money with its natural resources and tourism industry, why can't the government educate its children? With income from its gold and petroleum, where is the money for the Ghanaian schools? The government must find a way to give its young people an education through high school.

There should be a law that requires the government to provide for its young people. Children want to go to school. Some of the worst crimes against children in Africa are those whose political parties kidnap children to turn them into slaves or child soldiers.

Ghana boasts being rich in gold, diamonds, silver, and petroleum, but there are no financial aid or grants for the students. It doesn't make sense. For Ghanaian parents to put a child through school in Ghana, parents need courage, determination, and sacrifices. Parents are the same everywhere in the world—all parents want what is best for their children, but sometimes life does not go the way they plan and money is not available.

After a child is born in Ghana, parents have only five years to start preparing their finances so they can get their children in school. The greater challenge is try to find enough money to keep them in school all the way to the end of high school. If the hardships become too much for a family, their children's education will end. Family farms are crucial to a child's education, because the farms may bring in enough money to pay the school bills. Since so much time has to be spent on the farm, farm children usually have no social life at home after school. Sometimes, children come home after school to find no food to eat because mom and dad are away working late on the farm. As soon as children get home, they are taught to change out of their uniforms and go to the farms to help their parents. Sometimes, the children just eat corn on the cob or a little fruit and head out to help their parents in the fields.

In families who are very poor, often children are forced to go without shoes and must walk barefoot. However, schools do require that students wear uniforms while in school. I can say that God is so good because the many years I walked in the bush at my grandparent's village I survived without serious injuries.

The next sacrifice the poor families make in Ghana and other poor countries is the idea of three meals a day. If a student eats breakfast at home, the student may not eat again until dinner time. The dinner meal may not be big because whatever small amount of food the parents bring home has to be shared with the siblings. Children have no opportunity to be picky. They have to eat what their parents offer or go hungry for eight or twelve hours. Picky eaters do not exist among the poorer families of Africa. Every child in a poor family learns to be thankful for small amount of any food.

This fact is especially true for girls because many parents believe their daughters only need vocational training or no education because they will get married and have children. The false notion that girls only need to learn to sew and cook still dominates parents' decisions. Some families are willing to marry their daughters off and push them to start their own families with older men in order to avoid the school expenses. As long as these attitudes prevail, the country will be depriving itself of female doctors, care givers, politicians, and leaders that come from well educated citizens. All too often, female students finish their elementary grades, and after that, families are reluctant to pay any more to further their daughters' education.

As a child, I was eager to go to school and to make new friends. However, I began to realize that some friends would disappear and never return to school. I came to realize their parents had hit hard times and simply ran out of school money.

Photo credit: Emmanuel Taah

Figure 13   Boy forced to work instead of going to school.

Photo credit: Emmanuel Taah

Figure 14   Without enough education, women may resort to selling food on the street.

CHAPTER 8

RELIGIONS IN GHANA

Wisdom today: The radical religious extremists fail to see that their hypocrisy is devoid of divine love; simply said, their religious persecutions mock God's righteousness and love.

The Seventh Day Adventist (SDA) church was about two miles away from everyone's homes in my town. Since the church members were mostly teachers, farmers, and seamstresses, everyone was poor so no one could afford a car. It was customary to see about two hundred people walking to church on Saturdays.

My parents were raised in the SDA church whose missionaries came to Ghana more than 100 years ago to establish churches, schools and some medical clinics. Those churches and nonprofit organizations become known as NGOs (Non-Government Organizations). Christian churches were some of the most organized and enthusiastic participants who wanted to help Africa. Christians came to Africa to follow one of the most memorable commandments Jesus gave his followers as recorded in the King James Version of the Gospel of Mark 16:15: "Go ye into all the world, and preach the gospel to every creature." Another translation (The New

International Version) reads, "Go into all the world and preach the gospel to all creation." (New International Version)

As SDA followers, we believe that God created all things and rested on the seventh day. That's why we worship on Saturdays from sun down Friday until sun down Saturdays, the customary worship times of Jews and Muslims after sunset. Of course, Christians have traditionally worshiped on Sundays. We also believe that God is in Heaven preparing a place where we will join Him one day.

The SDA worshippers believe in following these basic rules: no eating of pork (Old Testament teaching); no smoking (New Testament teaching by the Apostle Paul to treat your body as the temple of God); no drinking alcohol (Old and New Testament teachings about the dangers of becoming drunk); and dressing discreetly (New Testament teaching about being modest and not vain).

In the SDA schools, all the students had to obey the same rules, such as worshiping on Saturdays, wearing school uniforms, and being on time for school.

In Ghana, there are three main religions: Christians, Muslims, and the native African religions. Christians believe in Jesus Christ as their Savior who died for their sins, was resurrected, and in His Second Coming will take his followers to Heaven to be there forever. Muslims believe in Muhammad and his teachings. The traditional native people, known as animists, believe that all natural objects from trees to rocks have souls, and they use dolls to create gods. Some use leaves and parts of trees to heal people.

HOW LONG WILL PEACE LAST?

For centuries in Ghana, the religious groups have always lived in peace. Unfortunately, today's world has become more violent, not only because of genocide, but also because Muslim extremists believe in "purifying" the world by creating Muslim societies and countries where only Muslims live. The radical Muslims openly persecute, torture, and murder Christians who do not convert to Islam. It's difficult to understand that certain Muslims are beheading Christians, whom they call infidels, and gleefully play the role of executioner to punish these infidels in the name of Allah. The idea of freedom of religion and peaceful co-existence does not exist for extremist Muslims around the world. Some Muslims look forward to the day when they can destroy Israel, the western countries, and all non-Muslim religions. Over the years, India has had wars between Muslims and Hindus, adding to the fact that religious wars are nothing new in history. In recent years, radical Muslims have sought to conquer and control small parts of Africa. persecution of Christians is a tragic fact around the world right now; today it seems that radical Muslims have shown no tolerance for Christians.

We can thank God if Ghana remains as peaceful now as it has for many centuries. Ghana's major wars happened when foreign countries came to colonize the country. At this time, religious wars and persecutions have not infiltrated Ghana. The people of Ghana are peace-loving, so it is hard to imagine Ghana being overrun by radical Muslims bent on killing off half the population just because they claim to be Christians.

CHAPTER 9

TEACHERS, FATHERS AND ADULTS

Wisdom today: There are dedicated teachers who do not make very much money, but they commit themselves to helping the students be better citizens and learn how to have better lives.

As students in the Adventist schools, we had to obey certain formalities. For example, if a student went into the restroom and a teacher was already there, the student had to wait until the teacher finished and came out before going in. Schools were smaller, single-story buildings, so the teachers did not have separate bathrooms. Also, I think this rule may have been established to protect the students from any teacher who might be tempted to be involved in any sexual misconduct with students.

The students started their mornings by lining up outside to sing the national anthem and to hear the announcements before the students marched to their classrooms. Also, the teachers would check the students to make sure their nails were cut and their teeth clean.

The students followed another classroom rule: when a teacher entered, the whole class stood up to greet the teacher until the teacher told everyone to sit down.

I found through the years that more of the teachers were men than women. I can assume that men needed jobs so they were given preference over women teachers. Also, there may have been fewer educated women who were qualified to be teachers.

In the Adventist schools I attended, the teachers were allowed to use physical punishment—that meant using a cane. Furthermore, if the teachers knew the parents, they would go to the parent's house and tell them what their child had done wrong.

As for race, I never had too many white teachers because my schools were in the small towns. White teachers preferred working in the cities.

Since people believed that girls would get married and not go on to college, the teachers usually neglected the female students where there were both boys and girls in the same classroom.

When I attended college in America, I was surprised to learn that in America there were a lot more females than men in some classes. There is a definite cultural difference about female students in America, because I was surprised to see many females in America attending school, involved in churches, and out working. Times have begun to change today in Ghana, because more girls attend school, graduate from high school, and go on to college in the last 10 years.

I was taught as a child to respect and obey my father, teachers, and other adults. Ghanaian children were never allowed to argue or reject what their fathers, teachers, or adults said or wanted.

It is interesting to note that Ghanaian fathers used to take care of their nieces and care for them in the fathers' homes, because it was expected that nieces would take care of them when they were elderly. Thus, some fathers might neglect their own sons in order to have their nieces ready to take care of them. That attitude often created a big problem between fathers and their children though there was no guarantee that the nieces would take care of them.

In America, the adult children have much more of a say if they do not like something, while in Ghana, what the father says is what has to be done. Children were never allowed to challenge or disobey their fathers, teachers, or adults.

Since my teachers were mostly black males, I did notice the midwives were mostly white and were supported by the churches. They might have been medical missionary nurses who came from North America, Europe, and Australia to staff the rural medical needs of the people. Apart from the midwives, there were very few white people in the rural areas where I grew up.

We always need to thank our teachers and professors. Even when parents are frustrated with their children, teachers are always there to help children to learn and to prepare for a successful life.

CHAPTER 10

JUNIOR HIGH SCHOOL

Wisdom today: Learning lessons from tragedies can be as important as learning lessons from all our happy experiences.

After I graduated from the elementary grades 1 to 6, I entered Junior High School. It was only a public Adventist school. I thank God my parents believed in making sure we got an education. They knew that Ghana offered few job opportunities. Our education meant there had to be family sacrifices.

The junior high I attended was about nine miles away from my grandparent's village. To be closer to the school, I moved back to living with my parents in their town. Again, the government nor the church never provided a school bus service, so I walked several miles to school and several miles back home. Occasionally, a kind person would give us a free ride.

At this school, each student had to care for a patch that was his garden. Every morning at 8 a.m. students had to practice using a machete to clean and weed their gardens. Teachers inspected the gardens. If it was not clean, the student would get beaten with a cane.

Our fun activities included playing soccer and track. Playing was done in our school uniform because no one could afford buying separate clothes for playing sports.

I remember the beatings when students had not done their homework. Obviously, those students who were unprepared with their homework did not want to go to school. There were no excuses for being unprepared. Students who had not prepared the homework would get beaten on their backs with a cane by a teacher as a warning not to be unprepared again. It was part of our culture that any adult could discipline anyone's child if the child was not showing respect or doing something right.

Money was always an issue because all my classmates did not have extra money. In junior high, students were allowed to have a sports uniform. The poorer students could only afford to buy one uniform and that uniform had to last two years or more. It would probably be embarrassing to students in the U.S., but some of us were left wearing uniforms with holes from the wear and tear. We tried to fix the holes by sewing the holes. The school did require the students to wear their school uniforms. Without extra money, my classmates and I resorted to wearing our sneakers as long as they would last though some sneakers were falling apart.

Every church in Ghana has its own colors because they have their own schools. By the uniform colors, people knew which school the students attended. The junior high students were recognized for brown and yellow, while public high schools male students wore blue shirts and khaki pants, and the high school girls wore a checked dress. In addition, special colors, the religious high schools had the schools' name on the left chest and usually green and blue colors.

None of our parents owned washers and dryers, so the students were responsible for washing their uniforms by hand and hanging them outside to dry on sunny days. Some students had some bad luck when a cruel person stole the student's uniform which forced the student to spend money again to buy the required uniform.

The only memory of a tragic event in junior high happened one day when the students rented a bus and took a two-hour drive on a class trip to the largest natural lake in Ghana—Lake Bosometwe. Some local people had given an educational talk outside at the lake about the history and the importance of the lake. They had warned the students not to jump in the lake, but one boy started bragging and saying that he knew how to swim. He took off his outer clothes and jumped in the water. Time went by, but he never came back. The local people were forced to look for him. Unfortunately, this boy did not heed the warnings and wanted to show off to the other students or the girls. When the locals found him, he had drowned. That was the only trip I went on. We didn't have enough money to go on other trips and my parents certainly did not want to send me on any trip for fear that I might get killed accidentally or even get seriously hurt by my own foolish actions.

CHAPTER 11

HIGH SCHOOL

Wisdom today: From my Christian education, I learned the importance of living a righteous life.

To start the Adventist High School, I had gone back to living with my parents, but even that changed. School was far away from my parents' home. There were no school buses. In order to get to school better, I moved in with an uncle, one of my mother's brothers, and his wife. On the weekends, I would continue my duties of helping my grandparents on their farm.

The students whose families could afford to pay the room and board had their children live on the campus, which avoided long walks to school, and provided them three meals a day. Most students arranged to live with a friend in the town. I had to walk to school and buy my food. I was living in the next town away from the high school, so I had to walk about eight miles round trip to school. Walking to school was something I had always done since starting school. Whether the weather involved heavy rain or excessive heat, I learned to make it through the worst weather in order to be on time.

One difference in high school was that students were given

an extra piece of clothing—a track uniform for running. If some students needed special help, the Adventist church would help with food such as rice, wheat, and some clothes.

I can thank God that through my youth I was a healthy child. However, something went wrong in my first year of high school. During a school break, I went to Takyiman, a large town, where I set out to be a shoe shine boy in order to support myself. I had chosen Takyiman because there were a lot of tourists and rich people living there. Like other poor children supporting themselves and their families, I used to sleep in a small five-foot-by-five-foot kiosk with three other children where a seamstress worked in the daytime. While in Takyiman, I developed an infection. The sun became too hot for me so I became sick. When it was obvious I was feeling worse, I was sent back home on a bus.

Without money to go to a medical clinic, my grandparents took me to a herbalist. He put some medication in my ear and nose. My body reacted with secretions coming out of my nose and throat. I lost weight and couldn't eat. It took about four days to have a bowel movement. I finally did get better after a week, but I continued to rest in bed. Needing time to recover, I never went back to the town that summer. Unfortunately, I never made the money that I was hoping to make.

The Adventist High School was a private school, so Christian devotions were part of the curriculum. The devotions made the students think about God and the importance of living a righteous life. I considered it a good high school and I believe the teachers kept the students busy with Bible studies, Bible quizzes, singing competitions, talent shows, and sports events. All the activities I believe helped to keep the students away from having too much idle time that could lead them into bad influences such as drugs, smoking, or carousing around.

As I found in the earlier grades, most of the teachers were men.

The high school had a good number of students. Unfortunately, students kept dropping out because the parents could not afford to keep their children in high school. I consider that a tragedy because the students wanted to stay and the parents did not want to take them out. In a couple of years, those children would have had their high school diploma, but it was not to be for the poor students. I realized how things can change in life and we may have to detour off the education road we had hoped to continue on. Tears were shed by some students who had to leave because their dreams fell through. They were old enough to know that they were likely to face a future of remaining in poverty. In the United States, a high school student needs that diploma to make more money in life. Imagine how much worse it can be for a student in Ghana to drop out of school.

Students in Ghana needed a lot of determination to stay in school because they had to go home to work on their parents' farms which provided support money for the school expenses.

In high school, I estimated half of the students were girls, although the majority were in vocational classes where they were taught cooking and sewing. My high school may not have had the largest enrollment, but I believe we had about 500 students and an average class size of about 40 students.

In addition to the vocational, the high school had two main departments: Arts where students were taught history, geography, economics, and English; the second department was science where students learned chemistry, biology, physics, and mathematics. Students were placed according to their grade, so those with better grades would go to the science department.

The school had a cafeteria where students could eat lunch. However, the school allowed the students who lived in the town to go home to eat lunch. I did not have money for lunch, so I skipped lunch and, sometimes, used lunch time to play soccer with my friends.

On Saturdays at sunrise, the dormitory students went to worship all day. The day students were allowed to walk home on

Fridays after school. In my case, I walked home on Fridays and went to the Adventist church Saturday mornings in the nearby town.

I remember one day while walking to high school. I had met a female classmate along the way and we started walking together to school. Her father who happened to be a taxi driver came along as we were about half way to the high school and with another two miles to walk. He stopped and had his daughter get in, but he left me there on the road to continue walking to school. I started crying. I couldn't understand why her father was so against helping me. He must have thought that he wanted to teach his daughter to stay away from boys and didn't want her to walk with any boy. I thought, if that had been my dad, he would have given us both a ride. Some people would take pity on me a couple of times a month and offer me a ride, but the vans and taxis that did come along were always full. I was determined to finish high school, so I had no choice but to keep walking in order to finish my goal.

CHAPTER 12

POLITICS CHANGE IN GHANA

Wisdom today: In the history of world governments, it can be said that dictators hurt their country rather than help it. Thus, dictators are ultimately catastrophic for a country.

I remember one dramatic incident on the street as I headed to my home town while on a school break. When I got to a bus stop, a soldier was also there waiting for a bus. I had on my school shirt, but I had changed my pants. The soldier turned to me and said, "I see you are not wearing your school pants. You have improper clothes on. I'm going to discipline you." I thought this was unnecessary and not against the law as far as I knew. He then said, "Do a push up." I said, "No, I'm not going to do it. He said, "Yes, you are going to do it." I said, "No, because I have not done anything wrong." It turned into a big argument between us. We stood there about twenty minutes arguing while waiting for the bus. There was a group of ladies there waiting too. When he was about to hit me, they started begging him to let me go. They yelled, "Let him go! Let him go!" He did let me go and that was my last bad encounter I had with a soldier.

By 1992, Ghana now had a new constitution. As a high school student, I had no awareness of politics and the importance of the new constitution. However, the constitution decreed that the government was divided among a president, parliament, cabinet, council of state, and an independent judiciary. That was significant because too often African politics had deteriorated into dictators, bloody wars, guerrillas, and coups d'états.

Since my family and relatives did not have a TV or radio, we did not know what was happening in Ghana's politics. All I knew was whatever I saw on the street. As a high school student, I was too young to get involved in politics.

The best thing about the new constitution was that it restored multi-party politics. At this time, Rawlings was elected as president and he would be reelected in 1996. Looking at what happened at this time, I am thankful that Rawlings helped initiate a new multi-party constitution. Many African countries had been ruined by presidents who turned themselves into dictators. Thankfully, Rawlings didn't do this. However, he did allow too much civilian abuse right on the streets by the military and the police.

At this time, Ghana was at a crossroads and something good did happen. We have to jump ahead to see how things turned for the better. Rawlings did allow for multi-parties and the 2000 election was won by John Agyekum Kufuor from an opposition party, the New Patriotic Party, different from Rawlings's party. Not only had Kufuor won the 2000 election, he was reelected president in 2004. These 2000 and 2004 elections were monumental in Ghana and African politics. They represented a peaceful transfer of power from one government party to another party without a war or a military coups d'état. Ghana was now considered a stable democracy. The word stability may not be appreciated as much in the U.S., but stability can mean a tremendous influence as to how much investors are willing to help a country develop. Even though my life by 2004 was headed in a new direction, it still meant a lot to me that I could count on my home country to establish itself as a peaceful country and to do so without the influence of a guerrilla war.

Photo Credit: Emmanuel Taah
Figure 15 Political rally in Ghana.

CHAPTER 13

LIFE IN THE TOWNS

Wisdom today: Hardships don't have to defeat us, but they should teach us that with courage and determination we can use them to help change our lives.

Growing up in Ghana, I was fortunate to live in a town at times that had underground water pipes to transport water. Where we lived there was a pipe that must have gone to a well, because we had to crank a handle to get the water started. This water source helped, but growing up years before I had to walk about two miles to get water and carry it back home on my head. Sometimes, there would be a lot of people lined up and I would have to wait a long time. Also, the bullies would fight to get their water before anyone else.

Photo credit: Samuel Kwarteng
Figure 16 Boy pumping for water

Also, the town had traditional backup wells for the general public scattered around town where people would drop a bucket and pull it up full of water. These were community wells for everybody and located throughout the town.

Mothers had to be strong because they often had to carry the water balanced on their heads while carrying their babies attached to their backs.

Towns were larger than villages, so the government provided paved roads in towns. They paved the main roads, but not the side streets. Outside the town, the paving ended and the roads became dirt. When it rained, the dirt turned to mud. The more it rained the thicker the mud and the more useless the roads became for walking or driving. On those days, cars often got stuck and that meant wasting time to dig them out. In the United States, there are gutters to take away the rain and not too many muddy roads.

Young people were constantly moving between their homes where they lived with their parents and a town where they could carry small items to sell.

In Ghana, thousands of people can be seen walking and riding bicycles all the time. As in most of Africa, everybody walks. A few people had cars. It can probably be said that cars belonged only to the police, taxis, the wealthy, some businesses, retirees, and the politicians.

Was life in towns more dangerous? Towns in any country have more people and more people means more criminals walking around. There were rumors that the larger towns in Ghana had their dangers. Children were more vulnerable to this danger because they could be easily tricked and kidnapped into the bush.

The common wisdom was that there is always safety in numbers. In the U.S., children used to be able to walk safely on their own. It seems that child kidnappings and abuse have been on the increase in the U.S. It appears that children in Ghana are still safer on the street than children are in the U.S.

The idea of headless bodies was true because some bodies without heads had been found near my junior high and high school. Supposedly, it was not the military doing it, but bad people.

If a king of a tribe or of a town dies even today, I would warn people and children to stay in groups and do not go alone into the bush. Bad people may be on the prowl to kill someone in the name of the dead king. The people used to call the headless killings awawamodwe (serial killer).

Photo Credit: Emmanuel Taah

Figure 17   One of the lucky places where there is a paved street.

Photo Credit: Samuel Kwarteng

Figure 18 A dangerous situation where a road is falling apart and is left unrepaired.

CHAPTER 14

PREPARING FOR GRADUATION

Wisdom today: Ghana could grow a middle class much like China has grown a new middle class that is now better educated and has money to spend on purchases.

In Ghana, there are three school terms each year. Students are given their grades at the end of the third term. On the final term, students either get a certificate of graduation or move to the next grade level.

In the U.S., students take exams along the way. In Ghana, students have to take one big exam at the end of each year. That means taking one test to pass or fail for the year, so students have to be ready for the big test and it puts them under a lot of stress to pass. Some students meet in small study groups at night to prepare.

There is a school admission fee and fees at the end of every term, so the fees have to be paid three times per year in addition to the admission fee. Along the way, there are other fees. If a student has to move to the next trade level, the parents have to be ready to pay a school fee every term before the student moves forward.

Again, the Ghanaian government is not investing in its children. I believe the government has the resources to invest in its citizens. Without well trained young people, Ghana does not have a good workforce. I believe that is one reason why Ghana does not have a middle class. As poor as China was at one time, it is obvious that they have a developing middle class and a middle class means that people have extra money to spend because they have jobs and a steady income. If people are not secure with getting or keeping their jobs, they do not want to spend. To see children and some adults on the street selling handkerchiefs is a sign that the people are not educated enough in order to hold jobs.

Many students pay an employer in order to learn on the job. In addition, Ghana now requires certain trades to pass an exam too. After a student passes an exam, the new graduate has to have money to pay for the license to work.

If I was still in Ghana, what would I be doing? I have seen my friends there lately and I see them doing nothing, only a few survive. We can thank God when He brings changes into our lives. Without changes for improvement, we can be stuck in poverty. People are willing to work to get out of poverty, but they need work opportunities in order to change their lives.

People may ask: why don't the churches sponsor all the students? The answer is: some students are sponsored, but the churches cannot sponsor the thousands of students at the same time. A sponsorship or education grant would be a miracle for any student, but how can a church or nonprofit take on the challenge of helping thousands of students every year? It falls back to the government with its gold and petroleum income to educate the children. The goal is a real education for thousands who need an education and the economic results will include a better economy based on new jobs and a growing middle class.

Photo Credit: Emmanuel Taah

Figure 19 Boys weaving in Kante.

CHAPTER 15

COMMUNICATING WITH OUR PARENTS

Wisdom today: People who want to immigrate to the U.S. or any country will need courage and determination to face new challenges of cultural differences, attitudes from others, and new financial expenses.

When I was fifteen, our parents moved to the United States. Dad had enough money saved up for Mom and him to fly to the U.S. They kept in touch with us by sending letters to the SDA church near our village. Their letters came two to three times a month. If someone in the U.S. traveled back to Ghana, such as our extended family of uncles or nieces as well as friends, they would bring us clothes and money. Twice a year, our parents would send us and our relatives in Ghana clothes they had bought. Our parents sent us shoes for church and sneakers for everyday wear. In Ghana, there were poor people around us, but we never had trouble with anyone robbing us for our clothes or shoes.

As for our parents' letters, they were written in both English and our native language—Twi (akan). Our Mom and Dad had to speak English at work in the U.S., so their native language had little use in the U.S. except in the Ghanaian churches. Their letters would encourage us about our opportunities to eventually go to the U.S. and how they wanted us to keep going to the SDA church so we would not go off in the wrong direction of drugs and crime. Sometimes, my Dad wrote how I should go to school for plumbing. I understood he wanted the best for me, but I was not excited about becoming a plumber. As children, we would write them back in order to keep in touch and to let them know we were okay.

Our parents wanted to bring us to the U.S., but they had no exact date. After all, bringing children to the U.S. could be expensive. There would be the costs of plane tickets, finding an apartment or a rented house to house us, public transportation, new clothes, and school expenses. To us, it seemed they needed a millionaire's budget.

Back in 1992 when our parents left, my grandparents did not have a telephone. No one in the village had a phone, including our neighbors and relatives. The only place with a telephone was the post office where there were three outside payphones. Our parents had to arrange a time with us when they would call so that we could be at one of the outside phones to get the call. We never used the phones to call our parents in America because we only had money for food. The long distance calls were too expensive for us to call. Phones were a luxury, so people often waited in long lines to talk to their relatives in other countries.

Photo credit: Rita Gyamfuah
Figure 20   Big Wheels Ghana Style

CHAPTER 16

LIFE AFTER HIGH SCHOOL

Wisdom today: Changes come in life, so let us be prepared for a better tomorrow by preparing ourselves for the coming changes.

With high school over, I didn't want to continue living with my grandparents with nothing to do. I decided I would learn to weave Kente clothes in a town where my parents used to live. These clothes, woven by hand and by our tribe in that town, had become known throughout Ghana. Kente weaving was mostly what the people do in the town. I had known about the Kente weavers back in junior high when I would watch the weavers and in time I began to learn from them.

Mom didn't want me to learn to weave because she was afraid I wouldn't want to continue in school. She used to fight with me all the time about spending time with the weavers. She had bigger dreams for me. As for me, I simply learned the special weaving skills to weave some clothes for a customer in order to make money. When mom caught me with the weavers, she always had a fit. Her message was "stay away and stay in school." After a while, I stopped going to the weavers to keep her happy and to concentrate on my education. In my heart, I really wanted to finish my education, but mom feared that weaving might tempt me away from school.

After graduation, I started weaving again. By now, our parents had been in the U.S. and mom could not stop me this time. I left my grandparents for a town far away to learn weaving. I would bring back pieces of clothing to my grandmother's village and sell my clothes there. I expanded my little business to about seven other villages where I sold my weaving and took new orders. I joined thousands of other Ghanaians to walk to all my locations. Although the small business required long hours, hard work, and a lot of walking, my weaving job was better than trying to sell ice water.

When I started my business, I lived with friends in order to save money. My work schedule went from 7 a.m. to 10 p.m. I started out as an employee. After six months, I had enough money saved up to be self-employed. The weavers had so many designs. When I went to the markets, I showed my samples and that's when people would give me a down payment to start on a design for them. They paid the balance when I delivered their finished job to them.

I did not believe that weaving was my destiny or my final job, but the job helped me to provide an income for myself and I considered I was doing better than selling ice water or shoe shining after graduation.

Photo Credit: Emmanuel Taah
Figure 21   Samuel used to do weaving before he could eat.

CHAPTER 17

PREPARING FOR THE U.S.

Wisdom today: The best families are those who experience a great joy in being together.

My siblings and I had been waiting and hoping for years that we would someday get a letter that said we could leave Ghana. That one letter of hope would make all the years of waiting worthwhile.

Since we had no personal phones available, our parents had sent us letters in care of our SDA church. The special letter we had waited years for came from mom. She told us to get ready. We had to take our medical tests. A small miracle was about to happen: our parents had the money to send us to the United States. We would be leaving our homeland of Ghana for the unexpected.

My siblings and I were living in separate places, but we got a message from mom and dad: we had to leave quickly. Each of us had to be interviewed at the U.S. embassy and accepted into the U.S. One of our uncles accompanied us to the embassy to talk for us because my siblings were minors. The embassy personnel interviewed us and didn't give us a hard time. Everything went smoothly for us to leave

Ghana.

After the interviews, the process went quickly. We got our visas in about two weeks. When we received them, our parents then bought us our airplane tickets. We picked up the tickets at the Cocoa House, a local travel business our parents had used to secure tickets. The people there would let our parents know when we were ready. In today's world, life is different because everything is done online so people purchase their tickets and simply go to the airport to pick them up. Back then, we had to pick up the tickets and bring them to the airport.

All the letters that came from our parents in the U.S. took about two weeks to reach us in Ghana. The delay in delivering the letters might have been with the mail system in Ghana. I don't know if anyone at the post office tried to see if money was inside, but it is known that post office employees in other countries do steal cash in letters that come from the U.S. Unlike America, mail was not delivered directly to homes. Churches which were a central part of everyone's life one way or another had become good collecting points for mail delivery. Many church members would go to church twice a day on Saturdays. The members worshipped all day starting at 9:30 a.m. and people would often stay until 6 p.m. Church was our life for entertainment, social connecting, personal improvement, and spiritual growth. Churches were often the lifeblood of a local village and a crucial part of people caring for one another.

In 1996, Rawlings was reelected as president of Ghana. I was now nineteen. It was a good time to get out of Ghana because Rawlings had turned the police and soldiers into gangs of thugs in his first election. I was nineteen years old and ready to take on the challenges of a new country. I had learned basic English because it was taught as the official language in our schools. Although I needed to learn American English, I was ready for America.

THE TRIP TO AMERICA

In June, 1996, my siblings and I took a bus to the airport in

Accra, Ghana's capital. We were eager, excited, and apprehensive all the same time. The four of us had never been on an airplane. We didn't know what to expect and could only hope that the plane would make it all the way for all those hours in the air. I prayed to God, "Dear Heavenly Father, if a plane is going to crash, please don't make it ours."

Along with our mixed feelings, we had a lot of joy. We would be seeing mom and dad again for the first time in about four years. To add icing to the cake, we would be living with them in America from now on. I think only immigrants can only really appreciate what it means to start over in America. American military personnel and anyone else who has served in poor countries are able to grasp how blessed America is. America is not a country to take for granted. All the freedom, friendliness, and moral qualities of America are interwoven into its culture, making it a great place, drawing millions of people to its shores. For what America offers the world, it's no wonder that Americans are proud of their country.

My siblings and I left our homeland at 11 p.m. on Ghanaian Airways for our ten-hour direct flight to JFK Airport in New York City. We traveled alone with no adults with us. We carried only one small suitcase for the four of us. Imagine coming as an immigrant to the U.S. with one suitcase. What would you bring? Shoes, clothes, pictures, a Bible, or mementos?

My siblings and I brought our personal Bibles. After all, we needed God to guide us in this new country. In addition, we brought our sponges we used to shower and only the clothes and shoes we were wearing. We only had the one suitcase because we knew we were not going back and we could not afford another suitcase. Any clothes we owned in Ghana we gave away for other family members to use.

We arrived in New York City around 10 a.m. on a weekday. It was nice warm weather. I was expecting cold weather and snow that dad had talked about in his letters for four years. He used to send us pictures of him wearing a heavy coat and standing in the snow. When we got off the plane in June, I was shocked that New

York felt like Ghana. I looked around. There was no snow. I said to dad, "You lied to us." My comment shocked him because he imagined we would be impressed with New York right away. He said, "What happened? What's wrong?" I said, "It's not cold. It's hot like Ghana." He laughed and said, "You wait and see." Mom was not able to be there because she had to work, but we would be meeting up with her after work.

We came with a few items in one suitcase, but mostly we came ready for what exciting things lay ahead in the United States.

Photo Credit: Emmanuel Taah
Figure 22   Fast food restaurant Ghana style.

Photo Credit: Emmanuel Taah
Figure 23   Seamstress applicants at a restaurant.

CHAPTER 18

GETTING STARTED

Wisdom today: An immigrant has the greatest feeling of joy when waking up for the first time in America.

Some immigrants are eager to start working after arriving in the U.S. We were still young, so an American education was our priority.

Our parents enrolled my siblings in public school within the first two weeks after we arrived. I was old enough to look for work, so my father took me to a nursing home where he worked in Queens, one of the five boroughs of New York City. He brought me there to say hello to his bosses and coworkers. After my dad explained my situation and the boss liked my friendliness, he told my dad, "I want to train Samuel." If I proved I could do the work, he would hire me. My supervisor trained me on the medication floor where I gave out medications to the patients. The medications had the residents' names on the bottles and I would administer their pills. Also, when the residents would be ready to eat, I would wheel them to their assigned seats at the dining tables where their names were listed. It was an easy 40-hour-week job. It was not difficult for me to be friendly to the patients, their relatives, and the staff. I proved myself to be friendly, dependable, and patient with the patients. After a month of training, my dad's boss agreed to hire me. I can thank God that I now had my first job in the U.S.

NURSING HOMES

Nursing homes were a new experience for me. There are no nursing homes in Ghana. As happens in poor countries, children have always had to take care of their elderly parents by having their parents live with them. Since nursing homes did not exist in Ghana, I found it interesting that my father and I were working in jobs that did not exist in Ghana.

U.S. EDUCATION

I still needed to get my GED in order to qualify for better jobs in the U.S. I began studying for my American GED at Touro College in Manhattan, but it was hard. By the time I got off work and took the subway and buses to the school, it was too late. My parents and I had already agreed that I would need more American education rather than my African high school diploma alone. I passed the test at Touro, so I was allowed to work on my high school GED and my Associate's degree at the same time. After I finished 24 credits at Touro, the school issued me a High School diploma from the New York City Board of Education. Then I continued my education at Touro until I completed my Associate degree in Science.

I found American English to be different from the British English taught in Ghana. Learning American idioms and slang made learning English more difficult. I suddenly realized I didn't understand American English and felt embarrassed. To protect myself from being laughed at, I spoke very little. I just remained quiet rather than appear dumb.

At work, the staff and patients thought that I was a very quiet person. The joke went around that the coworkers wished my Dad was quiet like me. I laughed and thought, "I don't know my English.

That's why I'm quiet, but you will see."

At our new apartment, my parents and siblings spoke our native language, but at work and at school I could only speak English. It took years listening and practicing the American English and the slang before I felt comfortable. Thankfully, Dad was not an absent father, so he was there encouraging us to keep learning and improving our English. With God's help, plus the patient help of our teachers and parents, we learned American English.

Photo credit: Donald MacLaren

Figure 24: The impressive **Verrazano Bridge between Staten Island and Queens, New York City.**

CHAPTER 19

A PLACE FOR OPPORTUNITIES

Wisdom today: One of the most precious things America offers is the belief that new opportunities are always available for every person who wants to try to change.

After I arrived, my dad once again began suggesting as he had done in his letters his idea that I should go to school to be a plumber. Plumbing was a hard and dirty job, required mathematical and mechanical skills, but it paid very well. A small plumbing company could bring in $100,000 to $500,000 a year. That kind of income was impossible in Ghana, unless someone worked as an executive in the petroleum industry, the cocoa business, or another top-ranking business.

I probably disappointed my father in his dream of a plumbing career for me. It was not a bad dream, but plumbing was not for me. In my own mind, God had settled what I should do in life. As a child, I had a dream where Jesus was talking to me—that I was going to be a postman and I was going to go overseas. After that dream, I wrote a little note to my mom about my bringing her overseas. She and I believed that we would not be staying in Ghana all our lives. I would pursue my God-given dream in childhood of working in the post office as a career.

As I grew up in Ghana, I used to go to the post office to ask about getting a post office job. That's where I learned a difficult reality about Ghana. It was not a country where you could apply for a job, pass a test, and be accepted. That was the process in the U.S. and millions of people got accepted to positions in the post office and other positions that way in the U.S. Ghana had a different process and presumably most of the poor countries operate the same way with their job applicants. You got a job in Ghana only if you knew somebody already in that job or company. The Ghanaian employer was not going to give someone a job just because they passed a test. It always took knowing somebody in Ghana before anyone could work anywhere.

This lack of opportunity exposes a major defect in Ghana's labor market. In the U.S., jobs are open to most everyone qualified. Job discrimination may exist subtly, but American companies advertise that they do not discriminate based on age, sex, race, and religion. It's against the law and most companies appear open-minded to all applicants. If an applicant passes a test, the person may get hired for an opening. Since I had no uncles, relatives, friends, or neighbors who worked in the post office, I would never get a post office job in Ghana. In fact, what company in Ghana would even hire me for a job without a college education or a specialized trade?

On the first day I arrived in the U.S., I asked my dad how I could get a job as a postman. He said I had to go to the post office and find out. I asked other young people and new friends how I could get a post office job. They would always laugh at me and made it seem as though I had asked them how to be an astronaut. Their answers were the same, "Are you crazy? There are people who have been here for years and they haven't passed the test. You're not going to get it because you won't pass the test." I said, "Well, I think it was meant to happen. I have faith and I know I'm going to get it."

After being laughed at by those who didn't believe in me, I

never asked my new friends again about the post office. I know that though the post office did not hold great status, I still believed in my dream as a child. With my dad's help, I learned what I had to do.

I was in America. This was probably the best country in the world to find ways to fulfill my dream. Probably tens of millions of immigrants came to America and said, "I believe in my dream and I'll reach my dream." That belief sustains immigrants through their most trying of times while adapting to America. I just kept seeking ways to fulfill my destiny until I got my job that literally came from my dream.

My advice to everyone: never let someone discourage you from your dreams. No dreams are small. Obviously, if I had wanted to be an astronaut, I would have had to plan a specialized science education and connect with NASA to pass their physical and other qualifying tests. If I had passed those tests, NASA might have had the first African and the only Ghanaian in space. Just have faith and do your part, and God will take care of it. God had put me in a place filled with opportunities—the U.S. That's what counted. Not everyone has to be a doctor, lawyer or astronaut to be where God wants them to be. Everyone has a place where God wants them. Are you ready for your opportunities?

Photo credit: Emmanuel Taah
Figure 25   Restaurant food preparation

Photo credit: Emmanuel Taah
Figure 26   Women selling corn to make money

CHAPTER 20

SOLVING PROBLEMS IN GHANA

Wisdom today: A country can improve and politicians are morally responsible to their citizens for improving everything the citizens need.

After settling into my new apartment in New York City in 1996, I reflected on my home country that I had left. I felt I was leaving the best and the worst in my African country. I hoped that someday my homeland would have many of the good things that Americans take for granted without thinking or worrying about what they need.

PUBLIC UTILITY: ELECTRICITY

In Ghanaian villages, there is no electricity. People rely on kerosene lanterns. If people don't have money for kerosene, they are stuck living in the dark.

When the American inventor Thomas Edison invented a light bulb that harnessed light, he opened up a way for the world to use electricity. Ever since that day, people preferred paying for the luxury of electricity, but most people still live in the dark. Electricity has become an expected and relied upon service to citizens in every country. Governments are judged whether they are any good based on their providing this service. Since businesses rely on electricity, they are unwilling to invest in a country if electricity is not reliable or available. Electricity is probably the most valuable invention for all mankind after the inventions of the wheel and the computer.

The Ghanaian politicians need to provide better electricity for their citizens, as well as the tourists and any businesses wanting to invest there. The Ghanaian politicians will continue to scare away tourists, retirees, and new businesses from coming. Considering the income from tourism and the natural resources, the politicians should direct money to improving the electric utilities. Good, reliable electricity keeps money flowing into the country.

There is electricity in the towns and cities. Not only do electric cutoffs threaten economic development, they cutoffs are also life-threatening when medical professionals and services cannot use their electrical medical equipment. In America and in other western countries, it's inconceivable that the electricity would suddenly cut off three or four times a day, but the failure of electricity has become a constant occurrence in Ghana. Besides the daily disruptions, electricity may disappear for hours, days, and even up to two weeks. How can a country grow when a basic utility is so unreliable? Although businesses have learned to have backup generators, the government still needs to care for the electrical needs of its citizens and tourists. And adding insult to injury, people may still be expected to pay a monthly electrical bill for the electricity they are not receiving.

Samuel Kwarteng experienced his first electrical outage in the U.S. in 2009—thirteen years after being here. Outages in the U.S. usually occur in localized areas, especially during bad weather. Ghanaians would be aghast to know how dependable electricity is in the U.S. They would say, "What! We have our electricity go off unexpectedly any time for seconds, hours or days." Having seen the reliability of electricity in the U.S., it would be nice to think that

Ghana would develop energy sources like solar and wind, the electric plants, and the infrastructure to provide dependable power.

While Ghana needs to make infrastructural improvements on many fronts, keeping the electricity flowing has to be a priority. American utility companies set the example: Electricity is a reliable energy source and utility companies get to work immediately if power goes out. That's the kind of get-to-it attitude that the Ghanaian politicians need to adopt. If it's necessary, let the Ghanaian government hire American utility consultants and engineers to solve the electricity problems plaguing Ghana.

PUBLIC UTILITY: WATER

In the cities, people have inside plumbing, but what good is the plumbing when the water may be shut off for four days or even a week or two? Lack of water is another major inconvenience. People cannot survive very long without water. Once again, let's remember, businesses, tourists, and citizens all need water. In America, there is a proverbial saying: don't shoot yourself in the foot. Without having a reliable supply of water every day, then it can be said that the Ghanaian government is "shooting itself in the foot." Money coming in from tourism and the sales of the natural resources should be available for the infrastructure utilities.

INFRACTURE: ROADS & TRANSPORTATION

In America, the elaborate highways and road systems are very impressive to any immigrant. During a car ride from JFK Airport to New York City, new immigrants get a good introduction to the vast array of roads, overpasses, bridges, and tunnels filled continuously with vehicles in all directions. Ghana doesn't even have a tunnel, because it doesn't need one. However, Ghana really needs paved roads. The existing dirt roads outside the cities can turn into horrible mud holes during the rainy seasons. That makes vehicle transportation come to a crawl or stop. Businesses need the

Ghanaian government to pave all its roads and build more bridges in order to have a prosperous economy.

TRANSPORTATION: PUBLIC

In Ghana, transportation involves private vans that drive around picking up people. Problems arise because there are too often too many people waiting for a van. The van schedules are unpredictable and when they do come, people have to shove others around them to get on. Just as in the U.S., buses are available for local and long distance travel.

There should be a better system for local transportation, including state sponsored buses. A better transportation system that keeps people moving has greater benefits for keeping the economy growing.

CARS & VEHICLES

Government officials are given their cars and chauffeurs, which shows the citizens that the politicians are taking care of themselves. The people simply want better roads, jobs, and the means to buy their own cars and trucks. Farmers would love to have a truck that belonged to a collective in their village so members of the collective could get more produce to the markets.

Ghanaian politicians are not helping their citizens as the laws do in the U.S. If a vehicle develops problems, it is recalled in the U.S. There are no vehicle recalls in Ghana. If an owner happens to find out his vehicle has problems, he has to pay to fix the problem because there are no laws protecting the consumer for helping the manufacturer pay for fixing the vehicle.

Some cities have emissions tests, but drivers may pay bribes to pass the tests. Ghana needs to start making new laws to enforce emission pollution and better vehicle inspections in order to maintain national safety standards.

Ghana is falling short regarding a notorious problem: drivers driving without a license or never having driving lessons. The unlicensed and repeat driving offenders manage to get away with murder in some cases because of bribing the officials. Ghanaian drivers are known to bribe the police and thus avoid getting tickets for speeding, having no license or having no insurance.

Photo credit: Emmanuel Taah

Figure 27   The future of Ghana is built on its students.

CHAPTER 21

CULTURAL VALUES AND DIFFERENCES

Wisdom today: To have a better life is everyone's dream, because you can not only help yourself, but so many others too.

The excitement of moving to the U.S. meant that I left behind a country radically different from the U.S. America made the difference from living in poverty to living in the middle class.

COOKING

Do you have a pot to cook in? In the U.S., unless someone is homeless, everyone can afford pots and pans for cooking. It's customary for people in America to show off their cooking talents. Men boast about cooking the best ribs, hamburgers, and meats on their barbecue. In the Ghanaian villages, most people don't have their own pot. They cook in one pot over an open wood fire and clean away any burnt section left in the pot so that another family can use that pot to cook at another time.

DIET

In Ghana, people typically eat spinach stew, plantain, cocoa, yams, lamb, goat, and chicken. Two typical local foods are Banku-fufu (cornmeal and plantain) and abetee-emotuo (dry cassava and rice). There are lambs and goats outside some houses where people can afford to raise them for meat.

As children, we learned to dig up worms in the ground and put them on hooks to catch fish in the rivers. People would also eat wild birds, but chickens were more popular. Chickens in the market cost money, so we only ate chicken once a year at Christmas. The chicken farmers could afford to eat chickens once a week, but most people could only afford to eat chicken once a year.

Christmas in Ghana is a time for a big family meal, more similar to a Thanksgiving meal in the U.S. Our family diet was limited to our parents' garden or farm. Rice was not common at the time, so we ate it occasionally. Ghana does grow rice and cows in the northern part of the country, and rice imported from other countries. Since fast food restaurants are not in the villages, we had no idea what fast food is.

MILITARY

The Ghanaian military does have an entrance test, but few young men get accepted. The old rule applies for the military as with any job: knowing somebody can get a young man in.

Ghana has one of the best military forces in Africa. As part of the African Union, the Ghanaian army is often sent to help keep peace in other African countries. In Ghana, there is no draft, similar to the U.S. Thus, young men are not required to go into the military.

Ghanaian soldiers have two basic jobs: protecting the country and disciplining the people. However, the soldiers do enforce a dress code on the teenagers which means teenagers cannot wear their pants hanging down as they do in parts of the U.S. The low-hanging pants actually came about in the U.S. because prisoners were not allowed to have belts in prison. Belts could be used as weapons against other prisoners. Thus, the loose-fitting pants would hang down. It became stylish in the U.S.. In Ghana, soldiers will stop a teenager and ask him to tie his belt tighter and keep his pants up. If he does not obey, the soldier is allowed to slap the teen with his fist and hit him with his cane. Teens may want their own style, but in Ghana, teens learn that they must look and dress respectfully.

HOMOSEXUALS

Homosexuality is illegal in Ghana. The Prime Minister of Uganda signed a law making homosexuality illegal, something still illegal in African countries. In America, conservative Christians oppose homosexuality, but a democracy has to allow homosexuality openly in order to be a democracy for all the people. In the U.S., people's freedoms override any religious constrictions.

TOURISTS & WHITE PEOPLE

Ghana is a popular African country for white tourists who enjoy nature-oriented travel. It is more common to see white people working in banks and at foreign companies in the cities. If a white person travels to a distant village, the villagers become excited seeing the stranger and the uneducated Ghanaians have an urge to touch a white person to find out how their bodies feel.

MOVIES

When I was growing up in the town, I knew that few people had electricity and even fewer had a black-and-white television at home. Those lucky few who did have televisions would charge rental fees to people who wanted to come over and watch their televisions. The owner might let the young children watch it for free, but would allow an audience on selected nights. This television was probably the only TV in town. The television owner was guaranteed to make money and people were willing to sit around for hours.

Thirty years ago, there were only a few regular TV stations. If someone had a projector, people also paid to watch Hollywood movies like *Rambo* and Akan (name of a tribe) dramas made locally. It was common to have 50 people in the home sitting there for the shows. Just like a theater, the owner would post a sign about a movie to be shown. People paid to go in. When a movie or show was over, people had to go outside. If they wanted more, they would pay again to come back inside to see the next show. This went on typically from 5 p.m. to 11 p.m. The movies and television shows were always a community event.

CAFÉS

Cafés are not popular in Ghana as they are in the U.S. or other western countries. In the U.S., people can be seen sitting around, relaxing, or using their laptops in Starbucks, Dunkin' Donuts, and other cafés. In Ghana, it has been the custom for people to cook their food at home and either eat at home or take the food with them. People in the villages have no extra money to indulge in the luxury of a coffee shop or café. In Ghanaian cities, people have better jobs or foreigners come with money so there are restaurants and beer bars. In the villages, people wait in long lines to buy rice and lamb or a local dish in front of some lady's home where she cooks and sells food out front of her home. The Ghanaian women have traditionally always done the cooking, not the men. In the villages and markets, some women cook the cheap and popular rice to make money. At other times after work or when traveling, people will buy food at a local stall along the street or outside from a homeowner in order to eat or take food home. The American fast food companies are more prolific in the cities now, but traditional home cooked dishes remain the mainstay of the Ghanaians traveling in the villages.

SMOKING

The social custom is for Ghanaian women not to smoke in

public. If a woman does, people immediately judge her to be a prostitute. Of course, not all women who smoke are prostitutes, but women with class still avoid smoking in public because it is frowned upon as a social breach of conduct. As long as young people live with their parents, they are not allowed to smoke or drink in their parents' home or in public. Once children are independent and living in their own apartment or house, they can smoke and drink all they want. The social mores in the U.S. allow women and young people of the legal age to smoke openly on the street.

CLOTHES & SHOES

Buying clothes is a luxury and not done as easily as people do in America. There are plenty of cheaper stores like Wal-Mart that cater to people in America, and American stores are always offering discounts and sales to draw customers in. The majority of Ghanaians cannot shop for clothes or shoes every year. What they buy has to last for years. It is common to see clothes and shoes sewn together and repaired multiple times. If there could be more jobs and just a little more income for the Ghanaian people, the country could be growing a middle class that could support a greater consumer economy.

HYPOCRISY

About 80 percent of the Ghanaian people claim to be Christian. Muslims form the country's second largest religious group. If people are involved with bribery and don't care about each other, what does that say about those who claim to be religious? Paying bribes teaches the people that they can buy their way out of going to prison and avoid responsibility. It's obvious that living together as a family or as a nation is not always easy. The only place where people will live honestly and peacefully is in Heaven. Until that time, let's minimize the hypocrisy, crime, and bribes that weaken the morals of any country.

STUDY ABROAD

Most Ghanaian students would like to study in other countries, especially in developed countries that offer better training, better research facilities, and better pay for graduates. In addition, other countries can offer reliable services and financial aid that in Ghana is not provided. It is called a brain drain when good students leave a country for better opportunities. The loss of good students impoverishes the country from developing faster and forces the country to pay money to outside consultants to help fix the recurring problems.

One major problem in Ghana already mentioned is the disruption of electric service, giving the country an F grade for this service to the people. The politicians need to gather the courage to help their students to get the highest education and improve the infrastructure. Let's make a suggestion: pay for the good students to study the engineering and sciences needed to improve the country. In return for their tuition help, those students would be obligated to work on government improvement projects for 10 years. Everyone would benefit with this education-government-infrastructure plan. This might be called the "Infrastructure Tuition Program." Students would be glad to make that commitment because they would have jobs and would be helping their country reach a higher level of production. That program would solve the brain drain problem which hurts Ghana from solving its many problems.

SOCIAL CLASSES

Ghana has two social classes: the rich and the poor. There is no middle class. At present, the wealthy Ghanaians send their children to private schools overseas or in special Ghanaian private schools. The brain drain can begin very early when parents feel a foreign education is preferred. It's natural for parents to want a better education and a better social mobility for their children. To have a middle class in Ghana is not asking for the impossible. The Ghanaian government needs to keep asking two basic questions: how can we help children to afford an education and to send some students to the "Infrastructure Tuition Program?" How can we keep improving our schools with better teachers and education tools, including books, computers, and labs?

America does have a middle class, though the middle-classes have been struggling financially more than they used to. The American Dream of owning a home with a white picket fence, a car, and having two children is harder to accomplish. Research has shown that the wealthy are getting wealthier faster in America while the middle class income has remained stagnant.

In Ghana, the economy is still a wide, long-term split between the wealthy and the poor. The poor are very poor, while the government workers and business people are living comfortably.

BATHROOMS OUTSIDE

In Ghana, bathrooms are not readily available, so people have to find a place to relieve themselves outside. Some men and women may stop near a building to urinate. It may seem strange to see the ladies going to one spot and the men and boys to another spot to urinate. It's against the law in America to urinate openly, but Ghana allows it because there are no public restrooms available. If there is a public bathroom, people have to pay to use it and pay for the toilet paper. Paying for a toilet and toilet paper is also done in Europe, not just in Africa. However, America has always had stricter laws about cleanliness and more bathrooms available for people. Also, people can use restaurant and other public bathrooms for free which are not available in Ghana. Overall, urinating in public is not a healthy practice for the people.

BANKS & MONEY

Banks in Africa are dangerous only because money can disappear or become hard to withdraw. Greeks learned this lesson when their banks only allowed the customers to withdraw $67.00 a day. That was a way of protecting the banks from defaulting and running out of cash.

In Ghana, small private banks may not give the customers all their money back. Big banks may pay a customer what was deposited, but the customer may get the money back slowly over days or weeks. The best advice in Ghana is to put money in the government banks and the bigger international banks.

In America, banks are better at protecting customers' money, but money is only protected up to $100,000. Another problem can arise in transferring money: If Ghanaian customers try to transfer money electronically from America to Ghana or between banks in Ghana, the receiving party will likely not get all the money. It's not right. This situation does apply to Ghanaian citizens. (This loss of money may not happen to the foreign residents, tourists, or visitors.)

The alternative to using the banks would be to send money with MoneyGram or Western Union. The author Samuel Kwarteng has used MoneyGram successfully for years. The nice thing is that money can be available for the recipient in 10 minutes. For the last 10 years, there has never been a problem.

As for Western Union, the author did have one bad experience. His wife had sent money from the U.S. while he was visiting Ghana. She paid her fee to send the money. That was expected, but then Western Union charged Samuel a fee to get the money in Ghana. There was a big argument. Samuel finally paid the fee, but he decided never to use Western Union again. However, Western Union has since changed its rule and does not charge a fee for collecting the money paid in U.S. dollars.

If people or businesses are considering the transfer of money in Ghana, it would be good to start with a small amount of money such as $300.00 to make sure there are no "unexpected charges," hidden fees or loss of money for any reason. It is critical that customers trust their African banks. If Ghanaian banks cannot be trusted, it's inevitable that customers will find ways to avoid the Ghanaian banks and move their money without losing it.

TAXES

In the villages, people do not pay taxes. People pay a little tax every day if they sell at the markets. Obviously, the tax rate in Ghana is far less than the U.S. tax rate. The lack of a basic tax system for Ghanaians hampers the government from collecting a fair amount of money from everyone. A fair, but simple tax system would help Ghana have better educational and social services for all ages. However, it takes honest leadership and oversight by the politicians to organize a tax system and collect taxes.

Lotteries are not recommended as a way to collect taxes, but it is interesting to note that Florida boasts on its state website that it has used over $21 billion in lottery money for educational purposes in the past five years. It is incredible the amount of money one state in the U.S. can collect by using lotteries as a form of tax income. Ghana will not hold lotteries as the states do in the U.S., but Ghana needs to use tax income for services for the citizens.

In the cities, tax collectors come to everyone's house once a year to collect tax money.

Those who pay taxes never get money back, unlike the taxpayers in America. In the U.S., people pay into the Social Security system in order to collect money every month later in life. At best in Ghana, a retiree might get a monthly sum or just be given a lump sum.

Most Ghanaians question whether their tax money is really benefiting anyone. Most agree that the taxes are not improving the needs of the citizens. They like to say: The government only takes, takes, takes, but never gives back.

People have a cynical belief that some companies may pay taxes, but they are likely paying more in bribes than taxes.

For those who own property in Ghana, the taxes are low compared to western countries. Property taxes are paid according to the date a person begins to build the house. A person with a house in the town might pay about $100-200 per year, while a homeowner in a village might pay about $50 a year. Overall, tax collection does not exist too well in Ghana.

TEENAGE PREGNANCY

Years ago in Ghana, a pregnant teenage girl would have to hide away at home and not go to school. A pregnancy represented the end of a girl's education. There was one girl who got pregnant and she came back to finish junior high. She was determined to finish high school and she did, although she got her diploma a year later than her classmates. Her struggle to finish was a big story at the time. On the other hand, pregnant teens in the U.S. are given a lot of support and schools help them finish their high school education. Most Ghanaian girls have in the past been afraid of public comments and ridicule for becoming pregnant, so their shame forced them to drop out of school. Attitudes have been changing in Ghana because there are classes today to help pregnant girls to get their GED. Abortions are not an option in Ghana because it is a dangerous procedure that could kill the young girls, and basically, abortion is not at all socially acceptable.

In extreme cases, some families will force the pregnant girl to have an abortion or just throw the girl out of the house. If the pregnant teen chooses to run away, she faces two options: becoming homeless or finding a family who might help her. Teenage girls around the world need to avoid getting pregnant, because a teenage pregnancy puts stress on everyone, especially in Ghana. In some places, there is a housing problem for pregnant teenagers and the government does not provide sufficient medical treatment. On the other hand, a few teenagers get pregnant on purpose because of the hardship at home, such as not enough food, so she looks for a boyfriend or older man to help her.

PARENTS

In Ghana, the father is recognized and respected as the head of the household and he is expected to provide for the family. In America, there has been the social problem of the absent fathers. In Ghana, the social norm is for fathers to stay with their families.

Traditionally, in America and Ghana, mothers mostly "stay at home." Staying at home in Ghana did not have the same connotation as it meant in America. Ghanaian mothers still spend the day doing chores away from the house: washing clothes, which usually involves going to the rivers, carrying water home from the rivers, walking to the markets to buy food every day, cooking all the meals, and taking care of the children, including carrying babies on their backs while outside all day.

In Ghana today, women in the cities have more opportunities to leave home to work in businesses and not do the traditional home chores all day.

Generally, the rule of thumb in Ghana today is that parents rule their homes. That means children must obey their parents as long as the children live at home with their parents, even though the children may be adults in their thirties. If a child or teenager disobeys an adult on the street, adults always have the right to hit or beat the child openly. Abusing a child is not acceptable, but hitting a child to teach a lesson is acceptable and a way of keeping a sense of social order, respect, and peace among the people. There is no waiting for parents to discipline their child. In fact, when parents find out that their child had been disrespectful on the street, the child would get a second beating at home to reinforce the message that obedience and respect inside and outside the home was the rule and social custom.

AGE 18

In Africa, children cannot leave home just because they turn 18. They leave when they have a job, money, and other necessities they can afford without relying on their parents. It seems to be a negative family practice in America for children to leave home at 18 or the parents believe it is time to throw their children out just because they turn 18. At that age, children do not have the education, steady job, and maturity that they need. Without a good foundation of a job and income, children can either be forced to move back home later to be a burden on the parents or they may end up in jail because they made the wrong choices.

Children who reach eighteen in Ghana must show their parents that they are ready to accept adult responsibility if they want to leave home. In the U.S., eighteen year olds have some adult rights to be on their own, although U.S. teenagers still cannot drink until age 21. In certain tribes in Ghana, the child has to have a certain number of cows, clothes or money. Children stay at home until they are ready. Since Ghana does not have many opportunities, children may stay at home into their thirties or forties. If the child is not ready, the child is not leaving. Ghana's social attitude is correct in one way because it requires a young adult to be responsible. Just because someone turns eighteen, the young person does not leave the family without means of support. In Ghana, it is better that young people stay with their parents so the parents can advise and encourage their children to do the right things. Ghana's parents make sure their children only leave when they are ready and not leave based on a chronological age. This social and family practice ensures that children leave only after completing their education and securing some type of work.

A BROTHER'S KEEPER

In Ghana, people are their brother's keeper, even if a person is not part of the family. People say hello openly to everyone on the street, while in the U.S. children are taught not to talk to strangers for fear of being kidnapped and sexually abused. If someone is in distress, Ghanaians will help. People don't wait until somebody asks for help. People care for each other.

At home, the social rule in Ghana is that a child cannot sit while an adult is standing. That would be considered disrespect. In the U.S., children are allowed to sit on the subways while adults have to stand. That custom is not accepted in Ghana.

If somebody is sick in Ghana, a neighbor feels responsible to rent a car and get the sick person to the hospital. In Ghana, there is no 911 to call an ambulance or the police. However, Ghana may now have a number for emergency calls. The emergency call service only works in the cities, but there may still not be a good response to emergency calls because there are not enough police cars or the police may be stuck in the constant traffic jams.

CHAPTER 22

THE FAMILY

Wisdom today: Parents do influence their children's lives. Our dad made right choices to make our lives better. Without our father making those choices when he did, our family would be stuck in Ghana today and we would likely be stuck there living in poor conditions.

BACK TOGETHER AS A FAMILY

It is very common in Ghana for families to split up so other relatives can share the expenses of raising the children. If someone's aunt or uncle settles in another town or village, the relatives would send their children to live there in order to have the children attend a better school or have some new opportunities.

Dad was smart enough to use his money the right way. He had a bigger goal to come to the U.S. and give the whole family a better life. Some of his coworkers used their retirement money to buy cars. Now, some of them don't have their cars because of accidents and breakdowns. Father made a right choice because our lives are better. My long-term goal is to take care of my parents the same way they have taken care of me.

Many immigrants don't come to the U.S. as complete families. My parents did not want to come to the U.S. and burden some U.S. families to take care of them and their children at the same time. I call it "God's time, not our time." God blessed our mother and father, so we came when they could take care of us themselves.

ADVENTISTS IN THE U.S.

As a family, we continued in our Seventh Day Adventist faith in the U.S. We had a lot to thank God for. He had opened a door to the U.S. for us which meant giving us a new start. That is what God is all about—offering people a new life. As Christians, we believe a new life starts with repentance and faith in Jesus. Jesus offers people a new heart. The Apostle Paul wrote in 2 Corinthians 5:17: "Therefore if any man be in Christ, he is a new creature: old things are passed away; behold, all things are become new." When immigrants come to a country, they find themselves with new opportunities to start a new life. That's how my family and I felt. We believed in one overall vision: everything new had come from God. It was no wonder that we went to church and thanked God for all the new things that He had given us.

There are six Ghanaian churches in New York City and perhaps hundreds of Ghanaian churches of all Christian faiths around the country. Some other popular Ghanaian communities in the U.S. include Texas, Michigan, Los Angeles, Philadelphia, Worcester, Hartford, Bridgeport, and Newark.

In Ghana, our local church had about 200 members. There were two full-time pastors—a senior and an assistant—to cover the whole district of ten churches. The SDA church members did tithe which paid for the pastors and meant a little extra money to help needy people.

As for the SDA churches in the U.S., they would ship over rice, cooking oil, food, and shoes. The local church members would then distribute the rice to take home to support their families.

Many churches in the U.S. now provide cafés or free or

inexpensive meals after church. It's an informal way for members and visitors to socialize. In Ghana, our church never had after-church activities because there were too many people and feeding the people would cost too much.

GHANAIAN WORKERS

Now that our family was in the U.S., we had the blessing of making money and saving it, something that was nearly impossible in Ghana. To make matters worse, Ghanaian workers usually get paid once a month. It's been said that some teachers don't get paid for a whole year. The government ends up paying the teachers one time for the past 12 months, but their pay may only be for three months. Why does the government do this? How can it expect teachers to pay their rent, eat, and survive? In some cases, the teachers have to rely on relatives, spouses, or friends to get by until the government decides to do the right thing and pay them. There is no slave labor in Ghana, but not paying the teachers and other workers on time becomes a form of delayed financial slavery.

Paying workers once a year is another case of hurting the citizens for no good reason. Workers get demoralized and they leave the country to work in another country. The notion of "a fair day's pay for a fair day's work" and fair treatment are basic human standards that the government should practice. Governments should set the example and show that they treat all their citizens and workers fairly. The reputation of a country comes down to how it helps its people.

One big difference between here and there is that workers in the U.S. get paid weekly or bi-weekly while Ghanaian workers get paid monthly of every several months.

PENSIONS

In Ghana, only government workers receive a pension. Even though the farmers, fishermen, and all other workers are the backbone of the country, there is no pension or Social Security

System to help them when they retire. Without a proper retirement system, the government takes its share, but gives nothing to its retirees. Back in his time with the Great Depression and so many unemployed, President Franklin D. Roosevelt saw that the federal government needed to establish a social contract with the citizens so that they would be provided for in retirement.

My parents, siblings, and I are thankful that labor and retirement laws have already been established in America. These laws insure that we have some money when we retire.

It might be enough to say that we had made the trip to enter the U.S. But even more important, we were automatically granted rights as an employee, and the government could not take away our pensions as has happened in some foreign countries. For the first time in our lives, we had the government of the United States protecting us and making sure we were paid properly on time. Unfortunately, there are politicians in some foreign countries who think they can get away with crimes against the citizens.

Photo credit: Rita Gyamfuah

Figure 28   Fast Food Ghana Style

CHAPTER 23

BACK TO MY DREAM

Wisdom today: Dreams can be fulfilled in America. That is the promise and the reality that helps to make America great, not only for the citizens but for all immigrants who cannot fulfill their dreams anywhere else.

After arriving in June, 1996, two years later in June, 1998, I took my first post office exam in Jamaica, Queens, New York City. I failed.

I had been telling people, "I'm going to take the post office exam." They said, "Are you crazy? People who have been here for years don't pass it."

I finally had had enough negative comments telling me to give up. I stopped telling others my business. ADVICE: It's not always good or necessary to tell people what you want to do because they may discourage you. They may be mistaken while thinking they are giving you helpful advice and protecting you from the pain of failing. Failure is part of life. Failure can happen many times before there is success. Ask any inventor, research scientist, or billionaire how many times they experienced failure. Actually, others can help you more by warning that failure may happen, but you should still keep trying. That advice is better than all the negative advice such as, "give up the idea." If someone doesn't try to learn from failure, how can anyone achieve a dream? My friends should have taken the time to help me study for the next post office test, but they didn't. Now, alone on my own, I set out to fulfill my dream.

In September 1998, I started Touro College in Manhattan at nights while I kept working my day job at the Queens nursing home where my father introduced me in 1996. Going to school for me meant a lot of subway travel back and forth from Queens after work to Manhattan and back home to Queens. My youngest sister attended and graduated from high school in Queens.

My other sister and brother attended high school in Manhattan.

COLLEGE

The U.S. offers students a lot more in terms of grants and loans than many countries in the world. The best advice for school-age children is this: stay in school, do what's right, and be educated for the future. Better educated students can help to transform a country into a better place. Governments and politicians are too often shortsighted about students. They fail to understand that better students result in a better economy.

In Ghana, the new president cancelled the allowance for the training colleges and universities that had been promised by the previous administration. Imagine what each country could achieve if the politicians got serious about tuition-free education and top-quality supplies provided to students and schools from tax support.

In Ghana, young people usually give up on an academic education in order to become apprentices in sewing or carpentry. Although technical schools exist, they cost too much. What good is a country if its citizens only shine shoes, sell ice water, or become porters? However, the government should not take the attitude the students be damned, because the greater good of the country comes from what its citizens are doing.

BIRTHDAYS

One of the first cultural shocks in America had to do with birthdays. Everyone celebrates a birthday in the U.S. The day means cake, ice cream, parties, gifts, and cards. In Ghana, people have no money to buy gifts and have parties. Surprising as in may seem to Americans, there are no birthdays in Ghana. Birthdays are foreign to people in Ghana and likely foreign to the poor people around the world. Even now, the author does not celebrate his birthday with a cake and doesn't care about birthdays. Birthdays were never celebrated in the villages, but they have become more common in the cities where people have money. Poor families can only think about having some money just to buy food.

While living in the U.S., the author forgot it was his birthday. The people at his new job gave him a cake. Surprised to see a cake at work, he asked, "What is that?" People started laughing because he didn't know about birthdays. They said, "That's your birthday cake."

In the U.S., parents have more time and money to spend on their children, so birthdays are a happy part of the culture and children come to expect birthday gifts. In Ghana, it can be said that the child is not celebrated. A person can go through his whole life without ever hearing his parents say, "I love you." The Ghanaian people are more reserved which means they normally don't use hugs and kisses to show their love. Parents don't use the word love openly. Although hugs, kisses, and "I love you" are missing, children never feel neglected. Fathers may not have time to be part of their children's lives, but parents show their love by constantly trying to help their children. The better parents do anything to provide and to protect their children. That's a whole different way of showing their love.

CHAPTER 24

THE GOAL

Wisdom today: New directions in life may be delayed beyond our control or wishes, but seeking something new requires something from us—patience. Patience is always part of life's journey.

After failing my first post office exam in 1998, I was ready to try the exam again in June 1998. This time I passed. I was delighted and I believed God was helping me fulfill a dream He had given me. The only problem was that there was no opening. I had to wait.

In June of 2001, I was awarded my Associates degree from Touro College. I had not given up on my education. A job supervisor at the nursing home gave me books to read to help me with English. The teachers were nice to encourage me. When I read English, I had to translate it into my native language.

The first week of July, 2001, I got the call about an opening with the U.S. Post Office. Over the years, I learned to ask for transfers. If a new postal branch was not what I wanted, I was able to transfer to another one. By personal choice, I limited my postal work to two main locations: Manhattan and Connecticut.

A DREAM IN THE FIRST 90 DAYS

After three months at the post office, people were telling me that I would not be able to get Saturdays off. I needed Saturdays off so I could worship at my SDA church. Weekends off were reserved for those with seniority. As a new employee, I was expected to work on weekends.

I prayed to God to reason with Him, "I got to this country. You helped me to get here. You helped me to finally get my dream job. You can help me get Saturdays off." I knew God was going to give me the days off. I worked the weekends, but I continued to pray, "I know God, You will find a way to help me to get Saturdays off. If you do this, I will tell the world what You did for me."

One night I had a dream where Jesus Christ said to me, "I know you need Saturdays off to worship me. I will give it to you. Go to that lady and she will give you Saturdays off to worship me." I looked, but did not see the lady. He pointed His hand and it became fire. As soon as the fire started, I saw the lady. It was a lady I knew from my work, had never spoken to her, but knew her to be one of the supervisors.

The next day, I went to work, but I did not know how to approach the supervisor lady in my dream. I could not tell her about my dream or she would think I was crazy. I didn't talk to her. The second day, I saw her again, but didn't say anything. On the third day, she came to work in my area. She put me on route that needed three employees to deliver mail. This supervisor had three employees with her and kept me in the group while the other postal workers left on their assignments. When we started to leave, she told me to drive the car. She said, "Since you guys are late, I'm going to take you to lunch." She took us to a Chinese restaurant and fed us—four couriers and her. While we were eating, a voice said to me, "This is the time to talk to her. Tell her everything that you told me." During our conversation, she asked me, "How do you like this job?" I said, "I'll be honest with you. I love this job. My only problem is getting Saturdays off to go to church." She asked, "Why Saturday?" I said,

"All in my family are Adventists. We go to church on Friday nights and all-day Saturday. Now, because of the job, I'm the only one who cannot go to church with them." She asked, "What do you want me to do?" I said, "I don't know." She said, "You should go to the manager or the assistant manager because they are the ones who can help you." One of the employees at lunch spoke up for me, "But you are one of the bosses." She changed her mind and said, "Okay, I'll take care of it." We left and I did not think about what I had told her. Anything that could be changed was in God's hands.

Three days later, I was walking in the hallway when I saw the assistant manager come to me. I had never spoken to him and this was the first time he spoke to me, "Oh, you're the person I need to see." Right away, my blood pressure and anxiety rose because I thought, I'm a new employee. What did I do wrong? He said, "Come to my office." I followed him to his office. He explained, "Your supervisor talked to me and I explained that we don't give Saturdays off to anybody, especially someone new. There are people who have been here thirty or forty years and don't have Saturdays off. If I give it to you, it's going to create a problem. But something tells me to give it to you. Since you need it for church, I will give it to you. I want you to ask your pastor for letter to explain your worship situation. I'll keep it on file for you. I want the letter to be a witness so nobody can tell you that you can't have Saturdays off."

I brought a letter from the pastor and gave it to him. The assistant manager gave me Saturdays off. I have never worked on Saturdays ever since. Although I had only been there three months, God made it possible. As a compromise, I volunteered to work Sundays as a replacement for the Saturdays. The branch needed two people to switch for a weekend day off every other weekend, but I had volunteered to work every Sunday so others could have off. Everyone was happy. The message here is that God can make new things happen and He will take care of us. When I first started chasing my dream, everything seemed impossible, but with God all things are possible. In life, some people will try to bring you down, but don't take no for an answer. While people saw a barren woman in

Sarah, God saw the mother of all nations. When people saw David as a poor young shepherd, God saw a mighty king of Israel. When people saw Joseph as a poor prisoner, God saw a powerful prime minister of Egypt. Never mind what people see in you. Don't count yourself out. You are a great person in God's eyes.

NEW CITY SIGHTS

When I came to New York City, I was awed at all the highways leading away from JFK Airport. Everyone who comes to New York City is impressed with its many buildings, lights at night, multitudes of people, and its grandeur. For the first nineteen years of my life, I only knew dirt roads that turned into muddy roads in the wet seasons. In New York, I saw for the first time all roads were paved. When we went to Brooklyn, I saw bridges and couldn't help saying, "Wow, that's amazing." In America, there are bridges, tunnels, and paved roads leading everywhere. Some roads and bridges in the U.S. require paying a toll. In Ghana, there are tolls, but no one ever sees repairs being made. The Ghanaians cynically call the tolls rip-offs.

With the post office job, I was able to advance to driving the delivery vans. The only bad times for driving the vans came during rush hours and bad weather. I had traded the muddy roads of Ghana for the blizzards of New York City, but that didn't matter. God had made a new life for me. My old life in Ghana would have been worse than all the bad weather I would have driving around in New York City.

JOBS MAKE THE DIFFERENCE

What is nice about the U.S. is that a person does not always need a college degree to get a steady paying job. The police officers, child protective services, school safety, post office, and transportation jobs all pay well. Some of those workers have Masters degrees, but not all of them. The point is that the U.S. cares about its people. The federal and state labor departments are constantly checking the unemployment numbers and seeking ways to keep people employed. The economic health of a country depends on employment opportunities. If employment is so important in America, why don't the poor countries try to help educate their youth and find new job opportunities to help their economies? Jobs are too limited in Ghana. Once a student finishes college in Ghana, the young person has to become a teacher because jobs are limited. What can the Ghanaian politicians do to improve employment opportunities?

PRESIDENTS HERE AND THERE

When a U.S. president wants to start a project, a contract is drawn up and a commitment is made, so the next president continues to finish a project.

In Ghana, a new president usually stops any projects the former president had started. That means the former president may have gotten half way through a project and it is stopped half way under the new president. (This can happen in the U.S. too.) It doesn't make sense to leave highway repairs or construction unfinished that the former president had sponsored. Why leave infrastructure projects unfinished? Finished projects encourage more investors to get involved with a country that fulfills its goals. This is true for all African countries. It's no wonder that citizens become frustrated and complain that the politicians don't care about the people. African leaders should take care of the people and follow the good example of America. A caring government means a government by the people and for the people. The American Founding Fathers showed great wisdom when they described their new government that way. While each immigrant has the advantage of comparing America to the home country, immigrants' hearts ache when governments back home give up on projects that would help their citizens. Unfortunately, giving up on projects does happen. To get a glimpse of some of the unfinished projects in Ghana, the Appendix E will give readers insights into projects left to die.

Photo credit: Rita Gyamfuah
Figure 29   Sample Deco Home Style

CHAPTER 25

GLORIA IN MY LIFE

Wisdom today: Human love may not always be external, but God's love remains faithful forever. If you doubt that, then wait on God and He will reveal a lot more to you.

I met Gloria in a Bronx Seventh Day Adventist church. When new people arrive at the Bronx Ghana SDA church, the pastor introduces them to the congregation. I already knew two of her cousins in the church. When I saw her, something told me that that girl is going to be my wife. After the service, I went up to her cousins. Gloria was standing with them and I said, "Your cousin is going to be my future wife." They said, "Yeah, the guys are like that. You'll just take advantage of her and run." After that, I didn't say anything more, thinking they would not believe me and would become upset.

I watched Gloria to try to see what type of young girl she was. Two years later, I started talking to her more often. After a while, we began dating. When I started seeing Gloria, she was living with her parents in Stratford, Connecticut. I would go see her for lunch or dinner where she lived in Connecticut. Then she moved in with a teacher in Fairfield, Connecticut. I would take the Metro North train out of Manhattan to see her while I lived with my parents in Jamaica, a neighborhood in Queens, New York City. When I first saw Fairfield, it was spring. I loved the large lawns, the flowers spread out in front of people's homes, and the large porches. I thought this is a pretty place. I'm ready to move here.

By 2001, I decided to rent an apartment in West Haven, Connecticut. I invited Gloria to the apartment before it was furnished. I wanted to know if she loved me if I had nothing, but I was wrong. After we entered the apartment, I said, "I have nothing in my room." She said, "Don't worry. I love you for who you are, not what you have." She seemed okay with just me. A few days later, I moved my stuff into the apartment and brought her back. When she saw the furniture, she said, "Oh, you tricked me. You tricked me." I said, "I just wanted to see how you reacted when I had nothing to show you."

In keeping with our SDA Christian teachings, Gloria and I did not live together, but I lived in the apartment. I bought a used car to travel to work in Manhattan. However, the commute to Manhattan in the rush-hour traffic was too difficult and exhausting. I ended up taking the train to work and using the car on the weekends. Meanwhile, Gloria continued her studies in Connecticut to become a practical nurse.

In June 2001, I finally received my Associates degree. My life was moving forward in new ways.

In 2002, Gloria and I decided to have a traditional marriage that we would have had in Ghana. We could not go back to Ghana, but it did involve our relatives having a ceremony for us. Since my relatives did not have a home phone, I wrote a letter telling them about Gloria, our being in love, and wanting to marry. As was the custom, my relatives went to her home town to see her family. In Ghana, the elders of each family go to the other family to look around and inquire about their background. In other words, the relatives check out the family. After my relatives made their investigation, they approved and wrote back, "Fine. You can go ahead and marry her."

In October, 2002, Gloria and I could not afford the expense of a wedding, so we had a civil marriage in Connecticut. The teacher Gloria had lived with brought the lawyers for the small ceremony. Afterwards, Gloria and I moved into my Connecticut apartment.

In December, 2002, the traditional Ghanaian marriage ceremony was conducted without us in her home town.

In the following years, our family started to grow: In 2003, we first had our son Gabriel; in 2004, we had our daughter Hannah; and in 2008, we had twin boys, Shadrach and Gideon, all born in Connecticut and with Biblical names. The birth of the twins was not easy.

Four years after Hannah had been born, Gloria told me she was not feeling well. She went to the doctor and was given the news first. She called me and said, "I'm pregnant with twins." I said, "It can't be true. You're lying." She said, "Yes, it's true. They want me to come back in two weeks." I said, "Okay, I'll take a day off from work and go with you." I went with her to try to understand how this happened. The doctor was describing the heart and the parts of the babies looking at an ultrasound, but I couldn't see anything in the black and white images. I said, "Whatever you say. I have to wait until I see them. Otherwise, I'm not going to believe it." From early on, we knew twin boys were coming.

We now had the challenge of raising four children, but I was thankful I had established my career at the post office and could count on a steady income for my family of six. If we were living in Ghana, we would probably be living in poverty and trying to survive by having a farm. For whatever reasons, God had blessed us with four children who were born as citizens in the U.S.

CHAPTER 26

MOVING TO NEW YORK CITY

Wisdom today: Whether small changes or big changes, we can always say that God has places for us to be.

My wife and I decided to move to New York City so I would be close to my job and she could go to school to be a Licensed Practical Nurse. After the twin boys were born, Gloria and I began making plans for a move. We had the babies' dedication (baptism) at the SDA church. I had begun looking around in Queens that would take the six of us plus Gloria's mother who would be living with us. That meant seven of us in an apartment. I focused on Queens because it was a lot cheaper than Manhattan and there would be more green space.

My parents used to live in Kew Gardens, so I took their advice and applied for an apartment. When I saw an ad in the same area, I decided to look around. That's where I saw a sign of an apartment for rent. I met with the landlord and he showed me the apartment, but it was too expensive compared to what we were paying in Connecticut. After the interview, I went back home and told my wife, "It's a nice apartment. I really like it, but it's too expensive." Without any warning, we got a surprise call from the wife of the landlord. She said, "I like you. You have a good job. That is good. We are considering what we can do so you can live here." I told her, "Thank you very much for trying to help. I really like your apartment. Okay, so let me bring my wife."

Gloria and I went back the next Sunday. As soon as we arrived there, Gloria loved the apartment. We needed three bedrooms. I told the landlord that it was expensive, so he took $50 off. The rent would start at $1,500 a month. It was a good neighborhood and had good schools for the kids. We needed a neighborhood without drugs and shootings. As for transportation, the apartment was an answer to our prayers: Gloria could drive to work because a bus trip would take too long and I could jump on an express E train that would take me right to work in Manhattan.

Our apartment search was settled and now we would start life in New York City.

Photo credit: Donald MacLaren

Figure 30: A view of Manhattan across the East River with the United Nations on the right.

CHAPTER 27

SURPRISES IN THE U.S.

Wisdom today: With the invention of the airplane and the Internet, the world has shrunk into one large village where ideas are shared quickly, and we can learn a lot from each other.

Three of us in our family—Gloria, her mother, and I—used to live in Ghana. We knew, appreciated, and talked about the new surprises we had when we started living in the U.S. We would laugh and find it funny how we had quickly accepted our American lifestyle. There were a lot of differences we were learning.

WATER

One of the first things that struck us was having hot and cold water from the same faucet. Having indoor plumbing made life so much easier in America. If we still lived in Ghana, we would have to do what people there have been doing for centuries: boil water in a pot to get hot water. Since the water always got too hot, the Ghanaians have to add cold water to get it the right temperature.

Indoor plumbing was a miracle for us because we could easily adjust the water to the temperature we needed.

Back in Ghana, the three of us used to put a bucket on our heads, walk about five miles, and carry the water home. Some of our friends would ask us, "Was the water safe to drink?" There were no water purity tests and certainly no Environmental Control Department testing the water. We could only tell them, "It must have been safe or we would be dead by now."

SNOW

My first September was the coldest weather I had ever known. I caught the flu and was rushed me to the emergency room. I called my dad and told him, "I feel terrible. I think I'm about to die." He said, "Oh no, that's a cold or the flu." I asked, "What's a cold?" He said, "Welcome to America." They gave me antibiotics and I did recover, but I discovered how sore my muscles could be and how I had no energy.

Walking in snow turned into a new challenge. The snow came in December. The December cold air was unbearable. I used to cry when I waited in the cold for the bus. My ears felt like they were being cut off. I hated to wear a hat. I thought hats looked ugly on me. Dad said, "You have to wear a hat in this kind of weather or it can kill you." I put on the hat in front of him, but I put it in my pocket after he was out of sight.

I discovered that first winter one coat was not enough. I still felt cold, especially when the wind blew through the Manhattan canyons. In order to sleep at night, I had started to use two blankets. That first winter in New York I learned that dad had not lied to me. Winters were cold and some winter days were brutal with constant snowstorms blowing over the city every week.

EARLY WORK

I told Gloria and her mother stories about starting work in

my first American job. The first day of work dad woke me up and said, "Let's go to work." I said, "No, that's not fair." In Ghana, I had never gotten up early in the morning. Now in the U.S., he was waking me at 5 a.m. That early hour was new to me. I didn't want to get up. Sometimes, he would carry in a pitcher of water and threatened to throw it on me. Gradually, I got used to getting up early. I knew all along that God had given me a job in America. There were thousands of people in Ghana who had no work and they would have taken my job if there was a way. I thanked God for having my parents and having a job. I realized God was not going to give me a post office job right away, so I had to take what he provided and learn to say a prayer of thanks every night before I went to sleep. I knew I could not let my laziness at 5 a.m. destroy God's plan of helping me to get to a better place. I knew one job would lead to a better job. That's all I had to remember. As for the direction of my journey, I had to let God work that out.

CHAPTER 28

SHOP STEWARD

Wisdom today: Other people respect us if we just do what is right all the time.

While working in the post office Collections Unit in Manhattan, I had the opportunity to become a union Shop Steward in 2008. It's not an automatic position. A person has to be elected and elections are every three years. The opening came up because the Shop Steward at the time had to resign for health reasons. When I ran for the position, I was one of five candidates for two openings. Out of the five candidates, I'm proud to say that my coworkers trusted me enough and elected me to be a Shop Steward. The position meant representing them and fighting on their behalf. Having come to America in 1996, I had begun my career, achieved new dreams as the father of four children, and had now accomplished a new position as Shop Steward all within twelve years.

The Shop Steward does not receive too much pay, so a person has to have the motivation to represent the employees and the union.

Every station has its union representatives. The union gives me instructions and a detailed booklet of procedures to follow and every Shop Steward has to know the rules and the employees' rights. If a Steward doesn't know something nor has questions, the Steward calls the union office for advice.

Some people may not like to pay union dues and would like to think they don't need a union, but things happen, probably at every company. If there's a problem or an employee gets into trouble, the employee quickly realizes the importance of having a union fighting for him/her. Unions are a good protection and act much like lawyers. Americans are familiar with having unions protect them. The good unions fight unfair labor practices, harassment, or firings. The role of Shop Steward is a vital role in the organization. Therefore, it is important for the postal workers to vote for the best Shop Stewards in order to get the best results for protecting them.

Unfortunately, I don't think the unions in Ghana are helping the workers. In Ghana, I know a far worse stress that could have awaited me—unemployment in Ghana.

Considering all the financial difficulties the post office is experiencing in today's economy, the public still needs the hundreds of thousands of employees to pick up mail, not to steal anything of value, and to deliver mail around the country. I still believe in recommending people to apply for work at the post office because it is a steady job and mail delivery is a service that the government is obligated to provide. Also, I recommend people to use the USPS because it is cheaper than the private services, and has proven to be reliable since the nation began over 200 years ago.

CHAPTER 29

PARENTING

Wisdom today: Parents can be the best people in their children's lives and, though children may stray from their parents' teachings, children will still remember their parents as the foundation in their lives.

The following explains some of the significant differences of parents in the U.S. and in Ghana.

TWO PARENTS NECESSARY

The SDA church believes God made a man and a woman to produce children, so they advocate heterosexual couples in a home. Heterosexual couples represent a traditional family as presented in the Bible. With changing marriage and family laws in America, people are forced to realize that same-sex couples can raise children and have the same rights as heterosexual couples. Still, the SDA church believes male and female parents offer important gender differences for a child at home. In addition, the SDA church believes two parents in a home are better. Since gay rights do not exist in Ghana, Ghanaian culture teaches that families are made up of heterosexual couples as mother and father. Also, parents are expected to provide love and stability to their children, and not be abusive.

If one parent abuses the children, that parent needs counseling. If the abuse continues, it may be better for the parents to separate and the children to be raised with the parent that offers them more love. The golden rule is that a home should be safe place for all children and children should experience love from both parents.

PARENTS HERE AND THERE

In the U.S., parents are known to get their children involved with sports and various activities that encourage their children to discover their strengths and to express themselves. In Ghana, parents do not have the time or money to help individual children. A lesson from the U.S. parents: Ghanaian parents need to develop their children's strengths and find ways to help their children explore more than they do now.

In Africa, the parents do not encourage the child to express themselves freely. If a child likes to jump around, American parents try to put their child in a class and encourage dance lessons. The African parent says, "Stop or you are going to hurt yourself." The emphasis on the African child is to keep the child quiet at all times; African children may not know the talents they have until they grow up. The American parents encourage their child to do more. In Africa, the parents keep a child restricted and limited.

DISCIPLINE

In Ghana, people still believe in physical discipline. Thus, parents and any adults are generally permitted to spank a child or even hit a child with a stick. Ghanaian teachers have the right to hit the students with a cane as a way of teaching them to behave. Of course, some parents may request that the teacher not give physical punishment to their child.

Of course, physical discipline should not be so severe that it can be considered abuse. Abuse can be considered hurting the child to the point of leaving marks, breaking bones, or creating abnormal psychological attitudes and behavior. If a child is not confident or secure, it is possible that any physical discipline may lead to psychological problems. On the other hand, American parents run the risk of being arrested and having their children taken away by Child Services if someone sees them hitting their children in public. What may be culturally acceptable in Ghana is not allowed by law in America.

The goal in both countries as a rule is to allow parental discipline as necessary and parents need to find helpful forms of discipline as part of growing up. Physical discipline usually happens when a parent becomes completely frustrated with repeated misbehavior by a child and the parent wants to take immediate control of a bad child. Patience is not always available even with the best parents.

Parents from Ghana would likely wonder whether American children are being disciplined enough and taught to respect their elders. In the subways and buses, children usually do not give up their seats to the adults. In addition, teenagers and underage youth can be seen smoking in public. Without good discipline, children may feel they can do what they want.

Rather than choose physical discipline, parents need to use "talk education." Parents need to constantly talk to their children as a way of teaching them to show love and respect. Talk education by parents would go a long way to prevent problems. Without discipline and talk education, children may not know how to distinguish right from wrong. Ghanaian children are taught to knock before entering a room; to show respect by saying, yes, ma'am and no, ma'am; and to always say "please" and "thank you." And let's not forget to teach children to open doors for ladies. If parents don't discipline children, they will think it is okay to be bad. Then those children grow up to be a problem to the parents and society.

FREEDOM TO TRAVEL

In America, my dad was able to buy a car—an old Mercedes.

Although he took public transportation to work, we drove around a lot on the weekends, including to church and other places in Queens. In Ghana, my father could afford a car, but he saved the money in order to move his family to the United States. Coming to America, our parents worked hard and could afford almost everything that was not affordable back home in Ghana. To have a driver's license and your own car gives another dimension to the word freedom. Although Ghanaians are free to travel in their country, the lack of public transportation and the inability to buy a car in Ghana create economic limits that stifle freedom.

CHAPTER 30

PARENT GUIDELINES

Wisdom today: Advice for parents: sit down with your children and help them learn from you.

PARENT REMINDERS

My dad always told me, "It's going to be okay." That statement gave me hope and probably helped me to have a brighter outlook. When I got disciplined, my dad would tell me why I was getting disciplined.

Children come into this world without instructions. They should not be left to chance.

To be a parent, you have to make a commitment to your child and that ends up being a lifetime commitment of training. Advice for parents is something I learned in America: Hug your children. Hugging is not done in Ghana. We can go back to the Bible for good practical advice: teach your children the way they should go. A good path is never a path to be ashamed of following.

Although my parents were poor in Ghana, they took the time and effort to direct me to the right path. Parents need to give good examples to their children while they are young.

Some bad comments a parent could say to a child would be, "You should not have been born. You are a waste." Another bad comment a parent could say to a child would be "you are the worst thing that God created." Parents need to allow their children to be children and not discourage them. Some parents threaten their children, "If you leave, you are on your own." Instead, parents should keep teaching them right from wrong. Some children will disappoint their parents more than others, but parents should not give up on their children. A child who is not taught to succeed will likely come back with problems. Parents should not emphasize being dumb, but telling their children to use their God-given, unique talents.

STORY: A TEENAGER GOES BAD

Two immigrant families came from Ghana to the U.S. They had two boys and the boys became friends at age 14 while in high school. Unfortunately, the boys took the wrong path in life and became drug dealers. One ended up getting shot and killed at seventeen. The parents of the other boy, Jason, were scared for their son. They decided to send him back home to Ghana to live with their relatives, hoping that he would learn to be good.

In Ghana, Jason became worse because he had more freedom and nobody was taking the trouble to supervise him. He started dealing drugs there. Then he got five women pregnant in three months time. He had to provide for the women, so he started stealing. Jason and his friends got arrested for stealing in home invasions. His gang friends did not have money to pay restitution, so they ended serving jail time—one for two years and the other for three years. Jason's parents in America had money, so they sent the money, got him out of jail, and brought Jason back to America. He still had no job. He was looking for the fast money that came with selling drugs. Today, they are trying to get him to finish his GED. He could have finished high school in Ghana, but he took the wrong path there, too. Without his high school diploma, he has no future. If he is addicted to drugs, he will be on the long and very bumpy road of recovery. That road can have a lot of pot holes, meaning there could be a lot of setbacks for him.

Jason took advantage of being a foreigner from America. In America, an immigrant may not be accepted, but Ghanaians think foreigners have money. Also, Ghanaians would love for a foreigner to take them away to their country to live there, so Ghanaian girls go crazy over the foreign men.

Added to Jason's problems is the fact that his pregnant girlfriends in Ghana expect money from Jason or his parents. Therefore, his parents will likely have to send money to Ghana every month. Jason does have two older brothers still living in Ghana, but they have not made problems for themselves or their parents like Jason has done.

Children need to learn an important LESSON #1: In life, it's easy to get into trouble, but hard to get out of trouble. Therefore, children should always avoid anything that can bring trouble.

Children have another important LESSON #2: It's better to stay positive all the time. Positive attitudes and experiences can help avoid trouble. Another way of saying this type of lesson would be: Don't look for trouble, because trouble is always looking for you.

Some people made the mistake of having too many children when they were young. Even if they have good jobs and have divorced, a father is still responsible for taking care of his children. Boys should be taught that getting a girl pregnant is easy, but taking care of them is a challenge. Boys and girls too need to be taught one important word in life—responsibility, including financial and all the other responsibilities required for caring for a child.

Parents should not be afraid to give their teenagers advice before it's too late: Take the right path. Children should listen to their parents. If someone walks down the wrong path, that person may not be able to turn their life around—and the person could waste time being in jail.

Advice for parents: Teach, teach, and keep teaching your children to do right.

Children have to learn there are appropriate times for everything. There's a good time for marriage and a good time for having babies. Children gain wisdom by listening to wisdom. If a young person tries to do it his way, he may likely get into trouble. If a young person does not listen to advice, it may be too late and death can come too quickly in our violent neighborhoods.

A TEENAGER MAKES WRONG CHOICES

One of my classmates in Ghana had parents in the United States of America. They told him and his siblings that they were going to bring them to the U.S. He started messing around with the girls and got a couple of them pregnant. Because of his making wrong choices with the girls, his parents left him in Ghana and brought his younger siblings to the U.S. His parents were teaching him to be responsible for all of his actions. Having babies is a serious situation and he neglected taking responsibility for himself, the good of his family, and for the girls he hurt, including his babies.

There is one lesson in life that applies to everyone: whatever one does in life, there are consequences. If children decide to make the right choices, the consequences will help them to be better off.

A CONSTANT YOUTH PROBLEM – LISTENING TO BAD FRIENDS

One of the worst decisions a young person can make is to listen to his friends who may lead him astray. Teenagers soon learn that they face existential conflicts between right and wrong. Their parents may teach them to do right, but their friends may teach them to do wrong. A young person is making life-changing choices based on parents' advice and his friends' advice. It's very important for parents to know who their children's friends are. It may seem controlling, but parents need the phone numbers of friends and to know where their children are and where to find them when they need to. This helpful advice is not about controlling, but about preventing problems.

AFRICAN AND U.S. DIFFERENCES

African children learn to respect their elders and to seek their wisdom. The elders try to spend more time with the children in Africa. In the U.S., children and adults are overly focused on texting and their electronic games. Little wisdom for living is being learned or shared when people are focused on the electronic screens. Learning wisdom comes through human interaction, looking into each other's eyes to pay attention, hearing stories that teach, and discussing ideas. Let's challenge American youth and parents with this thought: there is no wisdom being taught when the young person is busy playing the electronic games and sending messages to friends. Families need to spend time together at the dinner table and learn to talk to each other without their cell phones and electronic games interfering.

STORYTELLING TO LEARN A LESSON

My late grandfather in Ghana would tell me "ananse sem," meaning wisdom stories. Before there were televisions, radios, computers, and iPods, storytelling was a way of teaching children. The older generations would pass on tribal stories and wisdom that they considered very important to a younger generation. Generations communicated in personal ways with visual words and dramatic stories, not through electronic devices. Children in America may actually be spending too much time texting each other and avoiding personal conversations. It's not just children. Research has shown that parents in playgrounds are more attentive to cell phone texting than watching their children playing and even aware of any dangers for their children.

In typical African fashion, my late grandfather told me about a lady who had five children. She loved four of her children because they went to school. Those four children got jobs—lawyer, teacher, police officer, and a pilot. Her fifth child was considered "a nobody" because he did not seem too smart, so he was not sent to school. He made himself a garden in the backyard. He would go to his favorite spot and sit there alone because nobody liked him.

One day this mother went to the bush and found a baby alone. She decided to bring the baby home to clean him up and give him a haircut. The baby's mother showed up and said, "My baby is not allowed to have a haircut. That's why his hair is always like that. Since you cut his hair, I'm going to punish you. It doesn't matter what anybody says." The lady went to the leaders in town and they begged her to take the baby back. She said no. The baby's mother wanted the mother who cut the hair to put it back on the baby's head. They tried putting the hair back using glue.

The mother with four children brought the complaining mother to her son, the pilot. He said, "Wherever you go in this world, I will let you fly for free. So, please let my mommy go." The baby's mother said no. The mother took the baby's mother to her son, the teacher. The teacher said, "I will teach your baby and other kids for free." The baby's mother said no. The mother took the baby's mother to her son, the police officer. He said, "You know I'm a police officer. I will help you and your baby if there is trouble." The baby's mother said, "No, I won't let her go." The mother brought the baby's mother to all of her successful children, but the baby's mother had said no. There was only one son left who was in his garden who was supposed to be stupid. The mother took the baby's mother to him in the backyard. The mother assumed that this son had nothing to offer. That son said to the baby's mother, "Okay, if you don't want to let my mom go, this is what I am going to do. You saw the garden and the ground that I designed when you came to me. You saw that you made footprints where you walked. If you will not let mom go, I want you to close up every footstep you left." The baby's mother said okay and she started filling in her footprints. She closed her footprint and stepped on another footprint. She closed and stepped on another footprint. She did that for the whole day. She became exhausted and said, "Please let me go. Your mother can have my baby. Let me go." The son who was considered stupid got the lady to cooperate and to take her baby and leave.

My grandfather explained his lesson for telling this story: Do not dislike any child because the "bad" child may be the one to help you.

In the U.S. and other developed western countries, it seems that children need to be encouraged to get close to their elders and to learn from them. If an elder in the U.S. tries to tell a child he is doing something wrong, an American child does not like to be told what to do or be reprimanded. The child prefers always say, "I know. I know." It seems that Americans have gotten away from having their children around elders and having the opportunities of communicating with them. There is a lot of wisdom, knowledge, and stories that elders can share with children. Children can grow I wisdom through interactions with people of all ages, not just their electronic devices.

MY LATE GRANDFATHER'S LESSONS

My late grandfather would always give us advice. The following are some of his favorite.

Whatever you do in this world, you have to be very careful because this world is big and you may not fit in.

- Don't think you can get away with something wrong.
- Whatever happens to you in life, it is a lesson, whether good or bad. You learn something from it and take that lesson in order to do something better. Whenever something happens to someone, you can say, "Oh, it is a lesson, instead of asking questions like 'why me?'"
- Do not trouble trouble, until trouble troubles you. Then you trouble trouble back. Wherever you go on the street, do not start trouble. If someone tries to bully you, then you have to defend yourself or tell an adult.
- In life, you have to learn how to support yourself because mom and dad are here now, but not forever.

- If there is a problem, do not run away from it, but fix it.

PASTOR'S LESSON

When I was around nine years old, I remember learning a lesson from the SDA church pastor. He was preaching about God blessing us. He warned that any negative comments people tell us may come to pass. Therefore, we should stay around those who talk positive to us. If we do something good to someone, they will say, "God bless you." That blessing will follow you the rest of your life.

I see a lesson here: Because of my always trying to treat others the right way, I believe others blessed me and those blessings helped me to become who I am today.

NEGATIVE PEOPLE

Negative people can make you give up. That's why people need to ask what God wants. He is negative only with those who hurt others and practice evil instead of righteousness.

LESSON: Do what you think is right. If a person follows what is right, God is always with the person who is doing what is right. In this world, there will always be naysayers, because some people overflow with negativity. Positive people around you will help you create positive results in your life.

CHAPTER 31

TEACHING THE CHILDREN

Wisdom today: Societies grow better when the young people want to do what is right and have a better in life for themselves.

Gloria and I started teaching our children at a young age to stay on the right track. We also taught them to be humble and to fear God. Without God, there is nothing you can do on this earth. These are some lessons and stories to share with American parents and friends that they can share with their children.

Lesson #1: Appreciate What You Have
We have goals for our children. That often means giving our children what we as parents never had when growing up. In today's electronic world, that can mean cell phones, iPods, computers, and televisions. When I was growing up, we had none of those things and it was a difficult time in Ghana. We were lucky to have a little food. All I had was a dream and that was to come to a foreign country

which turned out to be the United States. As a father, I tell my children how my cousins and I used to sleep in bamboo rooms that leaked in rain storms. The kids in America don't know how difficult it was in Africa. When my parents brought me here, I didn't want to take anything for granted. Children in developed countries really need to learn the meaning of appreciation. If everything was taken away, then children would appreciate more what they have. I teach never take things for granted.

As a teenager in Africa, it took me a long time to wear shoes because we could not afford them. Sometimes, parents in Africa have a hard time putting food on the table. So how could parents buy clothes and shoes? I did a lot of shoe shines and work as a child to support my family too. In the U.S., I took advantage of getting my education and found a thousand more opportunities here than I would ever have in Africa.

Lesson #2: Accomplish More

I want my children to do better than me. I encourage them all the time to go to college and get a professional education. I tell my four children all the time, "You can be whatever you want to be. There is no limit in the sky." Furthermore, I remind them, "You may not accept what I say now about staying on the right track and make something good happen in your life, but in the very near future you will understand what I said was right. If you do too many wrong things, it is harder to get back on track. Look at all those young people who have criminal records. How many companies want to hire them? If a young person does wrong, it may be too late to have a good life. Sitting in jail one day is a waste of one day where someone doesn't need to be or belong. Don't waste your time being bad. If you do what's right, you're doing what's right for yourself, not just for somebody else. (You're helping yourself.) If you do bad, you do bad for yourself. (You will hurt yourself.) By doing good, you will be helping yourself and your children too. In addition, our children will someday be in a position to help other children in the world, such as those in Africa, to do better too. The whole world is a better place when we learn more and accomplish more.

Lesson #3: Stopped by Police

In a lot of places in the U.S., teenagers have to face up to gangs. While I was growing up in Ghana, I was aware there were gangs. I thank God that I never got involved with a gang. I never associated with those kinds of people. I try not to be in the wrong place at the wrong time. At the time, I did not even know what drugs looked like and I didn't want to know, and still I don't want to know. As for guns, I only saw them in the movies. In neighboring African countries, young children have been kidnapped and forced to be soldiers. Thankfully, Ghana was a lot different and more peaceful. I was never kidnapped and forced to kill someone. When I took a trip to the market, it was "on point:" I had to know where I was going and come straight back home without lingering around. When church was over, I came right home. Even when I went to the store, I knew what I had to buy and came right back. I never took time to do what is called window-shopping or hang out.

In America, there has been a lot of news about police shootings. One common thread appears to be that young people either resist cooperating with the police or they try to run away. Of course, there are some bad officers who will use physical force and even shoot someone multiple times. Children should be warned to cooperate with the police and not to run. Teaching cooperation does not mean the officer is right. It is important that children put themselves in the officer's shoes. Therefore, they shouldn't give an officer a reason to feel threatened to the point that he wants to shoot.

Teenagers have been known to cause problems and to rob. During Mayor Bloomberg's administration in New York City, the police practiced stop-and-frisk. Young minority men would be stopped multiple times on the street and searched for drugs and weapons. The goal was to keep crime down.

I started talking to our children about the police. I sat all of them down, including our daughter and told them, "You know you are from a good home. When you go out there, you have to behave yourself. You don't want any problems. Don't associate with bad people. If you do, the results will not be good. The police may watch more closely people who are black and Spanish. They pick on certain groups of people. It even happened to me. As you get to be teenagers, you will likely be stopped by the police. Don't feel angry with them and don't make it a bad experience." I was teaching them from my own personal experience.

I had been forced to stop while driving one day by the New York City police in a NYPD van. The police got out and circled my car. They drew their guns and ordered me out of the car. At that instant, any one of them could have started shooting, claiming that they thought I had a gun. Once one shoots, all the officers shoot. I got out with my hands up. I heard an officer shout, "He's got a postal uniform on!" The police backed away. One officer explained, "Your car fit the description of a robbery suspect." If I had not had on my postal uniform, I could have been shot or detained a long time. The police checked my ID and let me go. Out of all the jobs I could have had in the United States, the one that involved a postal uniform might have saved my life. The police immediately relaxed when they trusted that I was a good guy from the post office. I only hope that the police in America will get better training so they will not be too quick to shoot to kill because not all blacks and Hispanics are bad.

Lesson #4: Police Tactics

Sometimes, I don't blame the police for their strong tactics. I put myself in their place. What if I was a police officer and a stranger was approaching me? I don't know the person. If the officer is not alert, someone can kill the officer. The police don't know who is who.

On the other hand, I don't know what kind of training the police have. In Ghana, the police are trained not to kill. That's why the police have the nightstick and a Taser to get a person down. With some of the police shootings in the U.S., I am left wondering: Why does it seem that some police in the U.S. shoot to kill? Why don't police shoot someone in the leg, rather than kill?

The lesson to teach our minority children is: don't run away from the police, but be polite to them. Give them the answers that they need. I have to tell the children: (1) don't run away from the police because the police will assume you have done something wrong or you are carrying drugs or a gun and (2) don't associate with the wrong friends. If your friend is a drug dealer, you may become a drug dealer too. There is an African saying: "Show me your friend and I will show you your character."

I don't let my kids go to a friend's house. When they become teenagers, I will need to know the parents of their friends, talk to those parents, and know their addresses and phone numbers. It's important to check out the parents too. I tell my children, "Some people think they are big shots and important because they have drugs and guns. Those two things are the last things you need to be successful in life."

Lesson #5: Meet the Police

When I'm out walking with my kids, they may say, "Hey, daddy, look at the policeman. I want to say hi to the policeman." I take the children over to the policeman and we say hello. When children are young, they even say they want to be a policeman when they grow up. Our children have always been friendly with the police officers they meet. It's good to teach children that the police are their friends. I tell the kids, "We need the police. Without the good police, the bad people are going to come and catch you or kill you. Because of the bad people, we have to lock our doors."

Lesson #6: Social Problems

The fact that some people are out of work makes for more problems, making some desperate enough to resort to crime. That gets back to education. The youth should stay in school in order to find themselves better jobs.

I've heard some people say, "The people born in the states don't want to work." This is another major difference between the U.S. and Ghana. The U.S. pays a person's bills and puts money in their pocket for being unemployed or disabled. In Ghana, there is no social support system. The goal is simple: Americans getting social support should not abuse the system. They should use any support to help them, but not depend on social support forever. Americans are willing to help others get a better education and start a new career if they are out of work. By starting over in new ways, a person in the U.S. can pick himself up. In Ghana, a person out of work may stay out of work for decades and only have a little family support.

Lesson #7: Personal Care Training

When it's a cold winter in New York City, I teach the children they have to dress warmly. I am teaching them how to survive and to stay healthy. The children have to learn how to take care of themselves. Besides dressing for the cold weather, I teach them to always wash their hands. Hand washing is one of the biggest things anyone can do to protect them from colds, flu, hepatitis, and other diseases. When children learn to take care of themselves early on, they will learn about healthy living and respecting others in order to avoid passing germs and viruses on to others.

Photo credit: Rita Gyamfuah
Figure 31 Nzulezu village on stilts

CHAPTER 32

LESSONS OF LIFE STORIES

Wisdom today: Talking with your children will provide them the wisdom they will need for the rest of their lives. Face-to-face communicating involves so much more than texting words. People need nonverbal communication with a focused attention level to develop rapport, and emotional support not accomplished through texting alone.

NO QUESTION IS A STUPID QUESTION

While I was in college, I remember a professor said to the class, "There is no stupid question." Students need to be encouraged to interact with their teachers and ask questions and learn all they can by asking questions. When I came to America, my American English was very poor, so I was a shy student. I had to learn American English and all the American slang that was like a language unto itself. I learned by listening, practicing, and asking questions. I encourage my children to always ask questions. They have the advantage of growing up using American English and slang all day. With that base of everyday language skills, they can go on to achieve more easily and more quickly.

One day in New York City, it was hot so I wore my post

office shirt and short pants to work. A customer walked up to me and asked, "Mailman, may I ask you a question?" I said, "Sure." I assumed she was going to ask me directions or a question about the mail. Instead, she asked, "Why do you have chicken legs?" I said, "What do you think? I have a chicken body." She meant my legs were thin. I wondered, Am I supposed to have turkey legs? Her question simply reminded me what the professor had said: no question is a stupid question. My parents were not big bulky people, so I had a small body type too. God gave me the legs that matched my body. Thankfully, I had food as a child and survived growing up. Some children experience malnutrition. In Guatemala, the news showed that the Indians feed their children beans and corn all the time, which results in malnutrition. Without a variety of food at a young age, children can be malnourished and stunted in their growth. In the United States, vitamins are usually added to foods, such as bread, milk, and salt (iodine), so children get some nutrition. In Ghana, two good things can be said about the food: (1) we eat a variety and (2) the food is fresh. We don't put food in a refrigerator. Refrigerators are more available today, but they can be expensive. In the old ways, people would get their own food from their farm, cook it on the fire the same day, and eat it. Malnutrition would arise if some parents had too many children and could not afford a variety of food. I answered the lady by saying, "These legs run in the family." What else could I say? I like this story because I use it as a humorous example that no question is a stupid question.

NURSE STORY (FACT OR FICTION?)

Sometimes, I tell my children a fictitious story in order to teach them a lesson. Some stories sound good if no one can tell whether they are true or not. I told the children that a registered nurse was trying to buy a car. Her assistant nurse was doing better than the registered nurse. Instead of living her own dreams, the registered nurse was trying to live like the assistant nurse. She wanted what the assistant nurse had. The RN went to refinance a car, but found it difficult getting the car she wanted because she did not have good credit. She prayed to God to be able to buy the car, but it did not happen. The RN talked to another friend who had good credit and asked her to co-sign for her. Her friend agreed and co-signed. The RN brought the car home. One day, the RN drove her new car to the assistant nurse's house to show off her new car. On her way home, the RN was involved in an accident and died.

I had a message for my children: instead of being jealous of others, why don't people pray to God to ask him to work with what they have? Maybe what another person has is not going to help you. God knows what to give you. Remember the message from Jesus that God takes care of every sparrow, so He will take care of you. God knows today, tomorrow, and the future. God knew that getting the car was not going to help her. That's why He did not answer her prayers. When you ask God for something, it does not mean that God has to give it to you. If it's not good, God is not going to give it to you. In this story, God knew that the lady was going to die when she got the new car. One of the first things children have to learn is that they need to pray to God and be patient to see if what they prayed for is God's answer. The answer from God may not always be yes.

Is this story fact or fiction? Fiction, but it serves a multitude of purposes for teaching.

ANOTHER STORY (FACT OR FICTION?)

A foreigner came to America for a better living since there was no future in his homeland. He was willing to take any job, so he started in Burger King and Wendy's just to make money to send home to his family members so they could use the money to buy a house or something. When it was time to retire, he expected he would go home to live there. He had gone on to do construction jobs in the cold weather. He even got pneumonia from working outside. Little by little, he sent money back to his brother in their home town in Africa in order to build a house back home. He stayed in the U.S.

20 years and then decided to move back.

He made arrangements to meet his brother at the airport and get the house key. When he arrived he was very happy to see his brother meet him at the airport in Ghana. On their way home, the brother said to him, "Now that you are here, there is no food to eat. Why don't we go to a restaurant to eat before we go home?" They stopped at a restaurant to eat. The brother who had just returned told his brother that he was going to wash his hands before he ate. He went to the restroom and came back. Before he ate his food, he prayed. As soon as he finished and was ready to eat, the owner of the restaurant came to him and told him not to eat the food. The brother from America said, "May I know why?" The owner said, "While you were in the restroom, your brother put poison in your food." He said this in front of the brother. The brother in Africa said, "That cannot be true." The owner said, "I know you did it. I saw you do it. If you don't think it's not true, why don't you guys switch the food? You eat your brother's and you eat his." The brother from Ghana said no, "I won't do that." There was a big argument. The brother in Ghana finally admitted that he put poison in the food because he was trying to kill the American brother in order to take his house he had built in Africa. He did not want to kill him at the house for fear that the police would discover what happened and put him in jail. If he died in the restaurant, people might think there was a problem with the food. The brother from America was a good Christian who used to go to church, so God was protecting him. God was protecting him from the evil act of his greedy brother.

Is this story fact or fiction? Yes, it's true. The brother from America took possession of the house and the brothers never spoke again. Since the evil brother did not kill the brother from America, the case did not go anywhere. In America, the brother in Ghana could have been put in prison for attempted murder. It can be difficult to understand a person. After 20 years of receiving money from his brother, he was still jealous and wanted the whole house for himself. In the end, the man in Ghana did not help his brother the right way and hurt himself too.

GOVERNMENT – THE VOTING

The reason the government gets away with doing bad things is that the citizens do not take things into their own hands. A lot of people give up voting. They feel it's a waste of time because nothing good will come out of it and the politicians will do what they want to do anyway.

My advice: you have to vote. Children need to get involved. A close vote may stop the bad leaders in their corruption. When the politicians see that the people are voting, they may change their attitudes and decide to help the people. There have been a number of governments whose leaders and the ruling party were voted out because the people voted for new leaders.

While on the campaign trail in Ghana, some candidates go to the villages and give the people money, matches, kerosene, cell phones, tablets, and laptops. Instead of those immediate needs, the voters really need to think about the bigger issues—their children's education, the infrastructure, such as the roads, and any issue that improves the country. If the villagers had good roads, the people in the village could get to the market which could help them make money to put in their pockets. Also, the promise of money by a politician is not really very helpful. It will not help the people live the way they want to live. Politicians need to offer villagers long-term plans for the villages and the country's future, not voter payoffs for voting for them.

Most Ghanaian presidents promise nothing for the students' education. They want the students to pay their own education bills. A lot of families cannot even buy their children's school uniforms. How can they afford to pay their children's tuition? This is why people start rumors that the politicians are only good at putting money in their own pockets. The citizens have to look to the long-term and vote for the politicians who offer specific plans to help the citizens.

Children should be taught to vote because voting has brought in new governments and voting offers a peaceful transfer of power. Some examples of the people exercising their voting power have been shown in India in 2014 when voters overwhelmingly chose Narendra Modi to be the new prime minister. He promised to get rid of corruption and bring in change. Ghana also experienced the power of the voters when they elected a new government without having a war or bloodshed.

CARE FOR CHILDREN

In Ghana, the problem is that parents love their children, but they don't do enough for their children as they should. On the other hand, American parents live busy lives and don't have time for their children. In Ghana, parents don't read to their children before they go to bed. Those Ghanaian parents who know how to read don't customarily read to their children or spend time with their children. The children are told to go outside to play.In America, I learned that reading to a child at bedtime is a good thing. In both countries, parents should be reading to their children all the time.

In America, some parents leave early and may not see their children until bedtime, while other parents may not even know where their children are.

In Ghana, it is still considered safe for children to play outside without fear of being kidnapped. Over there, people trust other people more than Americans trust people. Ghanaians have a reputation of saying hello and talking to strangers. The opposite is true in America. Life has become scary in America now because thousands of children have been kidnapped and killed.

In Ghana, the government doesn't do anything special to protect children. In America, children are protected by social services agencies, such as Child Protective Services, that protect them from abuse. These services will take the children away from abusive parents. There is nothing like that in Ghana. In Ghana, only the parents care what happens, not the government. In America, it's against the law to leave children alone in a house, but in Ghana children can be left alone. In Ghana, most people live with extended families so there is usually an older teenager or adult around.

America protects its children through Medicaid, Food Stamps, and social programs. In Ghana, there are no social programs for children or families. If a Ghanaian family has no money, they will have to struggle on their own or with whatever help other relatives can provide. That's life in Ghana. In Ghana, only a few children go to college. Most students who finish high school don't have money for college or a trade school.

The Ghanaian politicians have made claims that their education system is good, but the politicians end up sending their children away to school in foreign countries. The politicians love to speak what the people call "double talk" as they try to convince the people that everything is fine.

APPRECIATE AMERICA

In Ghana, people would do anything to support themselves and their families without any pension. With the poor job market in Ghana, the cost of living is very low.

Ghanaians who have managed to live abroad are willing to take any job. Most people work two jobs in order to pay their bills. Some people work those jobs while going to school to prepare for a better life. No matter what kind of work someone does, every worker in America gets Social Security, besides qualifying for food stamps, Medicaid, Section 8, and more. None of these social services are available in Africa.

In America, there are plenty of bridges, buses, subways, and alternate routes in case an emergency blocks a road. There are always alternate roads around the emergency. In Ghana, there are only a few roads, so people get stuck in traffic jams that can last six hours or more. Once drivers are stuck in traffic, there are no alternate roads to get past the traffic jams. Ghana may only have about 50 bridges over the roads. Long delays may force people to get out of the vans and start walking. The Ghanaians call the traffic jams "go slow." Traffic lights are only in the cities and don't always help. In America, if a driver misses an exit, a driver can get off at the next to turn around. If Americans travel to Africa or any poor country, they will quickly realize all the advantages they have every day.

COUNTRY DIFFERENCES

The major difference between life here in America and life there in Ghana is that there is no future over there. In America, many things are possible as long as people work hard and do not hurt their credit. Also, people can go bankrupt and rebuild their credit in America, but that cannot be done in Ghana.

A common complaint in America is that the rent goes up every year, while the minimum wage does not. In Ghana, people live in their own house and those in the cities pay very cheap rent. It is common in Ghana to pay rent two to five years in advance.

The cost of living is better in Ghana. However, the future is better in America for job opportunities, making money, saving money, and starting a business. A child living in Ghana with poor parents is only going to live a recurring nightmare of poverty.

School resources are limited in Ghana. As long as the limitations continue, those who can afford a better education will continue to send their children to foreign countries for their education.

Ghanaians are friendly people and it does not appear that Ghanaian teenagers have started killing other teenagers to steal their clothes or shoes. In the United States, there have been tragic cases where teenagers kill other teenagers just to steal their coats or sneakers. That's the difference between our cultures. Even if strangers walk by each other in Ghana, people say hello to one another on the street. In the U.S., people don't know if a stranger may be dangerous so they don't feel safe saying hello or making eye contact. This quiet-don't talk attitude among strangers in the U.S. can be seen in New York City on the subways and buses.

In a study of countries, Ghana ranked around eighteen as one of the friendliest countries in the world out of 138 countries. The people in Ghana are friendly and are willing to say hello to anyone, especially if someone is an obvious Caucasian foreigner.

Photo credit: Rita Gyamfuah
Figure 32 Riding the bull on a bicycle.

CHAPTER 33

SAMPLE TEACHING LESSONS

Wisdom today: Share wisdom and teach lessons to your children as long as you have them around you, because what you teach them can give them an early start for the insights they need to deal with life's challenges.

THE KING REWARDS A SERVANT - STORY WITH A MORAL

The story starts out with a young king afraid that the elder fathers in town would overturn him one day because they had more experience and wisdom than him. He decides to have the elder fathers killed. He issues a command to do that, so all the elder fathers in town are killed.

One young man is supposed to kill his father because the king commanded it. He doesn't. Instead, he lies to the king and says he did, but instead, he hides his father in the forest where he feeds and clothes him for years.

The king wants the people to fear him and bow down to him at all times, but he is nothing more than a bully.

In order to make sure the people fear him, the king wants to be dressed like a tiger. If someone crosses the king, the king kills him.

He would not forgive anyone. To find a tiger skin, the king's servants go into the bush in search of a tiger. They kill a tiger and prepare its skin for the king to wear. The king puts on the tiger skin and wants to look untouchable.

After a few days, the tiger skin dries on his skin; and he can't get it off. The skin starts itching and hurting him. The king wants people's advice how to get the tiger skin off. When he tries, his own skin starts to peel off. Unfortunately, the king cannot get any advice because he had killed the elders.

The young man goes into the forest to feed his father. He tells his father what happened to the king. The father tells the son to pour cold water in a barrel. The king is to sleep there. Once he does that, the tiger skin will come off. The young man comes back and tells the king what to do to remove the tiger skin.

The king follows the instructions and the next day the tiger skin comes off. The king is happy. The king asks the young man, "How did you get that wisdom?" The servant tells the king, "You told us to kill our elder fathers. I did not kill my father. I lied to you. I hid him in the forest and have been feeding him every day. When this incident happened, I went to him and he advised me what to do."

The king tells the young man to bring his father home. The young man brings his father back. The king then gives the servant and the father half of his kingdom as a reward. The servant receives gold, jewels, and land. The king knows that the elder saved his life.

The moral of the story: the elders do have good wisdom to share. Young people will always need the elders around them. Don't say they are old and turn away without listening to them. For a young person to say, "I know, I know" is not an answer. Young people may only know half the answer and that is not good enough. Young people should share ideas with the elders and parents because they know better from their own experiences. The Americans have a saying: Two heads are better than one. Notice how that saying has nothing to do with avoiding our elders.

DOING WRONG HAS NEGATIVE RESULTS – A STORY WITH A MORAL LESSON

A young female immigrant comes to America. Her idea is to use people all the time to get what she wants. She meets a young man in a big American city, who is from her home country. He is a good person. After talking for several months, they like each other and start a relationship. They then decide to marry.

The young woman asks her husband to help pay her tuition so she can go to a four year college to get a better job. He cooperates and pays for her education.

During this time, the young woman goes back to some property she had in their home country. All this time, her husband does not go back home to visit. The young man thinks that, once she finishes college, she can get a job and help him go to school to further his education. Over time, the young woman goes back home more often. The young man does not know his wife had started a relationship with another man in the home country. She then secretly marries the man over there who is now her second husband.

The husband in America does not have children with his wife. The wife grows fat, but she is fat with a baby by her secret husband. She has the baby in her home country and her secret husband takes care of it.

One day, the wife goes home to Africa again. She stays in a hotel with a new boyfriend. By now, she has two husbands and a boyfriend. She tells the boyfriend in the hotel that she only has about three days left before she has to go back to America.

After leaving the hotel, she has an automobile accident and is killed. There is a funeral in Africa. Both widowers (husbands) attend, but the husbands do not know each other. They find out the truth at the wake. When her husband in America goes to the funeral in Africa, he meets her African husband, the secret child, and his family. When everyone realizes what happened, everyone starts fighting. The lady's family does not know she had two husbands.

The moral: Don't think you can do something wrong and get away with it. Whatever you do has consequences. People will find out if you are honest or dishonest. Do you want to be remembered as a bad person who did bad things? God does not like a bad person. That's why He gave the Ten Commandments and other lessons throughout the Bible. Again, life is like a basketball. When you throw the ball on the wall, it will come back to you. It is a moral rule that is just as important as a rule of physics: every action has consequences.

Photo credit: Rita Gyamfuah
Figure 33   Kente Weaving

CHAPTER 34

MEDICAL CARE IN GHANA

Wisdom today: Plan ahead to make sure you are covered for all types of medical and dental coverage in foreign countries in case of emergencies.

In Ghana, the majority of people don't have a car, so, if they need to get to the hospital, a neighbor or a taxi has to drive them. Ambulances may not always be available in a town. When it's time to leave the hospital to recuperate after medical treatment, people without a car have to take a van and recuperate at home.

In Ghana and poor countries, people do not have Medicare, Medicaid, homeless shelters, or hospices for the dying. Foster care and other caring services mostly or only exist where they are sponsored by the churches.

However, there are some good things about Ghanaian hospitals.

1...Patients can hire a private nurse.

2..The government provides some large hospitals and they are good.

3..Doctors come to Ghana from other countries to do notable research.

4..Koufur, a former Ghanaian president, had been the first to provide health insurance for everyone. Other presidents have limited the patients who get enrolled.

HOSPITAL

In Ghana, the poor have to expect these limitations at a hospital:

1...No bandages.
2...Few beds. Pregnant women have to come early or they may have to lie on the floor.
3...A high mortality rate. Many people die while waiting for treatment.
4...Specialists are rare.
5...Only pregnant mothers about to give birth are allowed in the delivery room.
6...Visitors can see patients for only an hour. Hospitals have cleaning hours, so visitors have to leave when cleaning is done.
7...If a patient wants to shower, the patient has to bring a bowl, soap, and a sponge from home.

PREGNANCIES

1...Parents have to bring their own baby clothes for the baby.
2...Ghanaians who can afford foreign medical care prefer to go overseas for their physicals.
3...Pregnant Ghanaian women who are wealthy often prefer giving birth overseas. A different birth country can insure a better future by living in the other country and a place to escape to if Ghana should ever have a guerilla war.
4...Ghana allows for dual citizenship, a great benefit for choosing where to live and having the freedom to travel.

HOSPITAL PAYMENT POLICY

1...Clinics can force patients to pay. In one incident, a friend of mine didn't have the money to pay the clinic, so they left the needle in his arm until he paid them.

2...Be prepared to pay with U.S. dollars. One time while visiting Ghana, the local hotel would only accept U.S. dollars. Why is it that the government allows hotels and, sometimes, medical care to only accept U.S. dollars?

3...A retiree usually has enough money to pay for his medical care. The problem is with the local people who don't have dollars.

4....Patients are sent home as soon as possible to recuperate.

5...It's a "cash and carry" medical system. A patient has to have money up front. If a retiree is too sick to go to the bank, the patent will have to borrow money from someone and the sick person pays it back as soon as possible. There are no prepaid accounts where money can be saved for hospital expenses later on. If a patient needs someone to withdraw money from a bank for the hospital, the patient needs to know who can be trusted to bring the money back to the hospital.

6....In Ghana, all the medical expenses are paid by the patients, not by the government that can include the sheets and bringing boiled water to the hospital.

DENTAL CARE IN GHANA

Growing up poor in Ghana, we used to take plantain sticks, cut them, pound them, and add charcoal to the ends to make a toothbrush and charcoal toothpaste. The homemade brush and paste kept our teeth healthy and clean. Also, there is a tree in the bush that people sell in the market to make toothbrushes. People chew the end to make it softer and then use it to brush their teeth.

Most dentists in Ghana have been trained in the U.S., England, Canada, Australia, and Thailand. Ghanaian dentistry has improved rapidly in the last 20 years.

GHANAIAN BANK ACCOUNT

A person from the U.S. can have a direct deposit from the

U.S. to Ghana. That's important because foreigners or retirees living in Ghana are sure of having money available for medical or dental emergencies, as well as for short and long-term care.

Photo credit: Emmanuel Taah
Figure 34 Hospital clinic

CHAPTER 35

CRIME & PUNISHMENT: PART I

Wisdom today: Imagine how different the world would be without criminals.

People want to live in a safe country. If people do not feel safe, people are willing to move to other parts of their country or take desperate measures to emigrate in order to find a safe haven in a new country. As immigrants, those people may face new hostilities from the other citizens, but at least those escaping a dangerous place have hope that they and their loved ones will not be killed. When people want to live somewhere or retire somewhere, they consider if there is a place with a low crime rate.

The following pages are reflections about crime in Ghana.

FAMILY INCIDENT

A boyfriend had a girlfriend whose grandfather was going to die. They lived together and had children, but they were not married. Her grandfather's last wish was that she would come to his funeral as a single woman because her boyfriend was not recognized as a son-in-law without being married.

When the grandfather passed, the granddaughter's family insisted that her boyfriend still had to pay a contribution like other son-in-laws who are expected to pay for the funeral expenses. The boyfriend cooperated and gave them the money.

At the funeral, the girl's family mentioned the names of those who gave their money, but they did not mention the boyfriend's name. Also at the funeral, the girl had relatives there, two army soldiers and a police officer. They came while off-duty without wearing their police and soldier uniforms.

The boyfriend felt he had not been treated fairly after giving his money, so he confronted the girl's parents. He asked why his name was not mentioned. They told him he was not part of the in-laws and was not mentioned, just as the grandfather had requested.

The boyfriend asked, "If you know I am not part of the family, then why collect my money? I want my money back." They did not want to give it back. There was an argument. In Ghana, people have to rent everything for the funeral. The boyfriend took a couple of chairs and took them home. The boyfriend's plan was that, if the parents wanted the chairs back, they would have to pay him back his money.

A few days later, the police officer and the two army soldiers who were part of the girlfriend's family saw the boyfriend riding his bicycle on the street. They stopped him, pushed him off, and beat him up. He nearly died from the beating. He ended up giving the chairs back so he would not be beat up again. In Ghana, he cannot report the beating to the police because the girlfriend's relative works for the police and there could be retaliation.

The boyfriend and girlfriend are still together, but he is trying to separate from the girl. The complication is that they have children, but never married. The boyfriend is afraid to stay because her three relatives may kill him if something happens again.

The moral of this real life incident is that it is to abide by the rules rather than be in mortal danger. That is a good lesson in the U.S. too. Don't put yourself in a position where others will want to hurt you.

GOVERNMENT OFFICIALS

All the African countries have the same problems in treating their citizens fairly. Governments often allow the police and the soldiers to beat people if the police believe it will make people obey. The lesson is to avoid questionable situations so as not to be arrested. Getting out of jail in any foreign country could take years unless bribing the authorities is possible.

There was the incident when a U.S. citizen visited a South American country with his wife who was from that country. When it came time to fly home, the couple had boarded and was seated on the plane. The soldiers came aboard and asked the American to get off. His wife came with him as a witness. They opened and inspected his suitcase to search for drugs. The American never used drugs, so none were found. The American and his wife were allowed to get back on board and the plane left for the U.S. If the soldiers wanted to give the couple a difficult time, they could have detained them for no reason.

GHANAIAN POLICE OFFICERS

There are two major problems with crime in Ghana. First, the government needs to pay their police better and provide them with better police equipment in order to catch criminals and to cut crime. The government probably does not pay them well, so the police are forced to survive by taking bribes. Secondly, the government needs to hold criminals more accountable. Some criminals pay to be let free. Getting free quickly only allows those criminals to repeat their crimes.

Another problem arises because most Ghanaians do not know they can report police abuse. Even if someone reports police abuse, the complaint will not go anywhere because the police like to hide their misconduct. The U.S. police have had incidents recently where they have taken advantage of their authority and have abused innocent people. Since police abuse exists everywhere, there is a need to educate people about reporting the incidents of official misconduct.

A friend had an incident while riding a taxi in Ghana. The driver picked up a second passenger. When it came time to let the second passenger off, the driver tried to overcharge the passenger. The passenger, who happened to be a soldier in civilian clothes, took control. In retaliation, the soldier took the ignition key and detained the car and the driver for hours before giving it back. The first passenger was stuck and unable to get to his destination. Most of the soldiers or police in Ghana do whatever they want with people and get away with it. The soldier was supposed to report the driver to the police, but he took matters into his own hands.

If someone does you a wrong in the U.S., people can call 911. In Ghana, there is no effective 911 call system. The police will beat someone up first. Again, the police may not investigate one of their own because the police officer will just say he had to control the situation or he had to defend himself. In Ghana, there is supposed to be a new 991 number for emergencies. The problem is that there are not enough police in every town or borough. The police have districts in Ghana and it may take the police a long time to travel to a scene and by then it may be too late.

Police can seldom chase after perpetrators of small crimes. Thus, victims have to rent a car, catch the perpetrators, and deliver the perpetrator to the precinct. When the police do come for a perpetrator, the perpetrator may not be around, so the police leave a message for the perpetrator to come to the precinct to explain his side of the story. The person may or may not show up at the precinct, and the police may not care to follow up unless they think it is a very serious matter.

If a serious crime has been committed against a victim, the case will go to court. If it is a less important case, the case can get settled at the police station. Normally, the loser ends up paying something to the victim. The victim can get paid all the money he spent to settle the case, including the expense of renting a car. The police, sometimes, tell the people to go home and settle everything with the help of the chiefs or leaders. In those cases, the police will follow-up with the chiefs or leaders to see that things do get settled.

TWO WAYS TO REPORT A CRIMINAL: TRIBAL KINGS and POLICE

If someone has committed a crime against a victim or creates a problem, the victim can report what happened to the tribal chief or to the police chief.

If the victim wants the tribal chief to get involved, the tribal king would sit everyone down, including the witnesses. The chief would ask what happened and gets everybody's side of the story. When everyone is done, the chief and elders decide who is guilty. The guilty one has to reimburse the expenses of the victim, similar to what would have been done at the police station.

In Ghana, children are always seen as guilty by the police and the king. When a child and adult have a problem, the child is always wrong and the adults are always right. If a parent and child fight and are brought before the king, the king will ask them to forgive one another and to move on. The adult may be wrong, but the elders don't want to embarrass the adult in front of the children. They just want everybody to pass it off.

There are still tribal chiefs in Ghana different from the king who represent the tribe or the region. The king and tribal chief are not the same persons. There is a tribal king and a town chief. Every clan has its own chief. The king is in charge of all the chiefs in the region. Every tribe has its own king. Every tribe speaks a different language, so the tribes have their own king. I'm from the Asante tribe and we have our own king. A repeat criminal would see a chief, but he would be taken before the king if he continues repeating his crimes.

The elected leader of the country is the president. The kings have to obey the president and the government.

Foreigners in Ghana usually have a choice of going to the

police or the king to settle a legal or criminal problem.

POLICE BRIBES

Even though bribes could be considered unethical and criminal, some Ghanaian police officers do accept bribes. If criminals know they can bribe the police, then those criminals will continue to commit crimes and not worry about going to jail. The bribes are bad for society and only make people cynical about trusting police. Bribes are part of life in Ghana because the police know the government is not stopping them. Drivers who own cars know to carry extra money because anyone who drives a distance in Ghana will be stopped along the route by one or more police officers, resulting in having to pay several bribes to those officers. By not paying a bribe, the driver runs the risk of losing time at the precinct or even going to jail on some flimsy excuse by the officer who didn't get paid.

POLICE CONFISCATE (AND MAYBE STEAL)

Normally a new business owner wants to rent a store, but many Ghanaians cannot afford to pay rent. Their alternative is to set up a table and start selling their items on the street. The authorities (police) have the reputation of taking advantage of the small business people. The police will confiscate (also known as steal) the items and beat up the street vendors. In Ghana, once the police take someone's items, the vendor may never get them back. Obviously, that's not only unfair, but illegal in any society.

The police, sometimes, may be willing to give back what they confiscated, but the vendor will have to pay the police a high fee. That can be called extortion. If the fees are too high, the vendors will have to walk away instead of paying the "fee."

In Ghana, the streets are filled with street merchants because they cannot afford to rent a store. The police come around every minute looking for targets as to who they can decide to close down. The government should stop this police extortion because successful small businesses can grow into larger businesses that can pay taxes to help the government.

It would be better for the government to use the incubator centers that specialize in helping business owners stay open. In addition, the government needs to develop a tax system that helps all business owners. In the U.S., the government has business incubators and a multitude of advisors to help small businesses to get started and to survive. Ghanaian politicians should follow this U.S. model to help small business to thrive and stop the police from randomly shutting down or stealing items from small business owners.

CHAPTER 36

CRIMINALS

Wisdom today: Criminals should never be allowed to get away with their crimes because not only can they hurt and murder victims, but they can financially ruin their victim's lives.

ROMANCE SCAMS

One favorite scam is to try to connect unsuspecting men into romantic scams with women in order to steal their money. The popular romantic scams on the internet could be called "I want to marry you." Men may pay for women to fly to meet them. The woman in the scam may let a man fall in love with her and then have a multitude of reasons why she needs financial help. Some scam requests might include: my mother has cancer and she needs medical help; I want to bring my sister to America too; I want to buy land in Africa where we could build a house. When it comes to marriage, any man or woman has to be wary of the many scams that can come along before committing to marriage. In the worse cases, a couple may marry only to find out that the bad spouse never intended to remain in the relationship.

CRIME – STOPPING CARS & ROBBING PASSENGERS

Some criminals in Ghana may not be carjackers who steal cars, but there are robbers who stop cars at gunpoint and rob the passengers. The majority of time the drivers are let go, but drivers need to have money hidden in the car to pay either the police bribes or the crime bosses who rob them along the road. The government needs to crackdown by having soldiers actively patrol the roads to keep them safe.

CRIME - GUNS

According to Ghanaian law, the public is not allowed to sell or buy AK-47s, but those are the kinds of guns the robbers are using. Apparently, those guns are available on the black market. Robbing at gunpoint is becoming worse and worse in Ghana. By the time the criminals have robbed someone in Ghana, the criminals are gone and the police cannot catch up to them. Also, the day may come when terrorists with guns will present a security problem in Ghana.

Too often, criminals spend a short time in prison and are back on the streets. Ghanaians do not have guns as people in the U.S. do, but Ghanaians may want guns to protect themselves and their families.

A reporter once asked a government official about there being too many guns in Ghana. The official said, "If a person thinks the country is no good, then the person should get a passport and leave." This attitude is not a solution to the growing gun problem. Politicians need to support the police and root out the criminal black market. This story can be seen on the internet.

CRIME - DRUGS

The most common drug being used in Ghana appears to be marijuana, still illegal. The U.S. is undergoing major changes in attitudes about the freedom to use marijuana. Although there are laws against the use of marijuana, some people claim medical marijuana offers them relief from pain and other symptoms. One detrimental problem of allowing the free use of marijuana comes when a driver high on marijuana cannot make safe decisions while driving. Despite the good of medical marijuana, Ghana will likely not relax their restrictions on marijuana

.

CRIME - KIDNAP

Criminals everywhere want fast money. Kidnapping may be considered too much trouble by some criminals. However, criminals in Ghana will try kidnapping someone who appears to be wealthy and worth the effort. Kidnapping is already an established crime and seen as a big business in Mexico and Colombia. If someone is kidnapped in Ghana, it is best not to resist or the kidnappers may become impatient and kill their victim. A common kidnapping scenario would be for two to ten men to invade a home and start shooting. Once the people are subdued in fear, the kidnappers demand money. There are two possible solutions to this crime: (1) pay the money and later ask the police to investigate and (2) have a highly sophisticated security system for the home and the car that may prevent intruders. However, people are always more vulnerable to kidnapping on the roads, in some parts of town, or in the bush where there are no police nearby. Criminals can catch their victims and release them after being paid.

CRIME - HOME INVASIONS

There are home break-ins in Ghana. This could involve one criminal or a gang of criminals similar to those who kidnap their victims. The difference with home invasions is that the payoff is immediate. Criminals steal whatever money and valuables are in the home and then escape. If criminals feel the victim(s) have not given up everything or they could identify them, the criminals may kill the victim(s) right away. The best way to secure a home from robbers and home invaders would involve good locks, electric surveillance cameras and recorders, and a common sense awareness when something or someone appears to be dangerous. Electronic systems and cameras are important, but homeowners need backup generators so the electronic security system will always work during electrical outages that could last for days.

CRIMINALS TODAY

There seem to be more criminals today than there used to be twenty years ago. Now, criminals may have more access to guns which make them bolder and dangerous. Tall walls around a house and heavy gates in the front may help deter crime to some degree, but determined criminals can scale the walls and get in unless a homeowner has an electronic security system. Ghana may not always keep good records about crime, so it can be difficult to find out what is really happening. In the U.S., anyone can go on the internet and find the crime statistics for a neighborhood as reported by the police and FBI. It would be very helpful if Ghana kept such records, but such information could prove that the country is not as safe as politicians claim—and that information could be very embarrassing.

PRISONERS

Young people in every society may do something wrong that results in their going to jail or prison. Jails may be defined as short term, while prisons are long term. Being locked up in jail or prison should be seen as a total waste of time. People should learn that trying to commit a crime is useless, because either the forensic evidence, circumstantial evidence, surveillance cameras, or witnesses are going to catch the crime. Jail or prison time is a waste of a person's life and the only lesson it teaches is that someone was so bad that he or she deserved to be punished.

However, young people in jail should be given one positive

message: do not think life is over. It may be harder to find work, because people will be suspicious about trusting a released prisoner.

In the U.S., people can stay in jail 20 years to life. Going to prison in Ghana is not going to be a fun experience because prisons are overcrowded, hot, and prison guards are allowed to beat up prisoners. Prisoners in the U.S. have more rights against prison guard abuse. In the US, the law does not allow the police to beat up suspects. However, the U.S. police precincts are coming under more scrutiny because of some bad police who have abused or killed suspects unnecessarily. In Ghana, the police are known to beat up a person whether a criminal or someone on the street for whatever reasons they want and leave the suspect to sit in his urine and excrement. In Ghana, if prisoners have money to pay a prison official, they are likely to get out of prison faster. Unfortunately, corruption is everywhere, including the prisons.

In the U.S., some prisoners are allowed to stay at home while wearing an ankle monitor that alerts the police if they leave home. Ghana normally doesn't use such sophisticated electronic systems.

As for bail in Ghana, someone has to put up their property as a guarantee. If the suspect runs away, the police will seize the property used for bail. Of course, the worse the crime, then the larger the bail will be.

Most people in foreign countries believe that American prisoners are pampered compared to the miserable, unsanitary prisons in poor countries. However, drug lords in some countries have been known to be given extraordinary privileges and freedom while in prison because they bribe and pay the authorities.

CAPITAL PUNISHMENT

Capital punishment does exist in Ghana and the authorities use either hanging or a shooting squad as the ultimate punishment.

REVENGE & PERSONAL JUSTICE

Revenge for an offense in Ghana often involves the victim hiring somebody to beat up the offending party. For example, there was a speeding driver who was stopped by some people who told him to slow down because there were children around. The driver got offended and hired some body builders. He had them come back and beat up some people in the neighborhood even though those beaten up had nothing to do with the original argument. The problem driver just wanted to make more trouble. It was not necessary to come back and beat up the people. When somebody in Ghana has money, the wealthy person can do what he wants and get away with it.

RIOTS

Riots don't take place in Ghana. Although the Ghanaians have legitimate complaints with the government, they do not riot. Of course, the government would never accept civil protest and end up sending in soldiers to squash any protests or riots.

One time in Ghana, someone saw a beautiful house and stopped to videotape it. The person who stopped didn't know who lived there and didn't see the soldiers sitting there. The soldiers came up to him, threatened to take away his camera, and beat him up. He defended himself saying that he did not see a sign that said no cameras. If he saw such a sign, he said he would not have started videotaping. They did not do anything because they probably heard his American English because in Ghana people speak British English. His accent probably helped saved him from losing his camera and stopped them from beating him up.

BRITISH COURT SYSTEM

In Ghana, the country once belonged to Britain, so the judges still follow tradition and wear white wigs in court. The only convenience for being a British colony in those days was that people were free to travel to Britain without needing a visa. People would just pick up a passport and go to England.

CHAPTER 37

SHOCKED

Wisdom today: It's always hard to predict how well a marriage will last.

In 2014, we knew a married couple, Raymond and Abby, who were Africans in the U.S. One night, Abby said she wanted a divorce. That was shattering news because they had been married for 12 years. Maybe it was naïve for the husband to think that everything was okay. Twelve years and three children later she suddenly seemed to want a new life.

They had their fights just like other couples. Abby had a way of not wanting to reason or compromise. In frustration or anger, Raymond would say, "Maybe one day I will leave you because what you are doing is not right. Someday, if I leave, I am not going to come back."

Fights make people say the wrong things, but angry words do express someone's frustration. At times, Abby was headstrong and wanted to do something that Raymond didn't agree with. Raymond and Abby struggled all the time especially with the stresses of three children and expenses.

Abby gave Raymond a hint a week or so before her divorce

statement. She told him she had a dream that they were no longer married and that they were divorced. Maybe she did not have such a dream, but the "dream" was her way of preparing him for the divorce.

Sometimes, people are warned not to marry someone, but they love the person and go ahead with the marriage. Before a couple marries in Ghana, the parents or relatives meet the woman's family to discover if the couple should or should not marry. Since Raymond's parents lived in the U.S., they were able to meet Abby already in the U.S., too. After meeting her, Raymond's parents did not demand that they should not marry. They simply warned him to be cautious because people are unpredictable, but they accepted their son's wishes if he wanted to marry her. In America, statistics show that about fifty percent of marriages fail. In Ghana, it's hard to find the statistics of failed marriages. The government probably claims it does not have the money to do social research about marriages, families, and divorces. The closest hint about divorce in Ghana may come from the number of divorce applications filed, but some people may divorce without filing for the divorce.

OTHER WARNINGS

While Abby and Raymond owned a house in New Jersey, they rented a room to a young man, thinking his rent could help pay part of the mortgage. He became a close friend, but he confided in Raymond that Abby was telling him a lot about their personal business. According to him, she planned on leaving Raymond after she finished school. Also, a neighbor told Raymond she heard from the same young man that Abby supposedly didn't love her husband. At the time, Raymond didn't want to believe any such gossip. Maybe others were warning him. He was happily married, went to work, and took care of his family. All along he thought they were okay as a couple.

Raymond had some friends in church who told him, "You will have to be careful with her." They only knew her from church, but not from their home country.

Raymond and Abby had not rushed into marriage. When they did marry, it seemed that Abby did not want him to be close to his relatives. Also, he felt she was trying to create problems with his friends. That way, he would have nobody to go to when she would leave him.

Raymond had discovered over the years that Abby could be headstrong. In other words, whatever Abby said had to be done, like a bossy person. She never seemed to cooperate with anything or be diplomatic. Things had to be her way, period. Other people could see and hear that, and told Raymond about it. She could defend herself saying, "I just want to do what's right for the family." However, it seemed obvious that it was her family—mother and relatives—not her marriage family. Abby's demands only created tension for Raymond. In time, he had to concede she had a need to control—everything.

In addition, Abby had a temper when she wanted her way, so they had unnecessary fights about small things over the years. He considered her bossy while she accused him of being bossy. In one example, Raymond preferred she should dress more modestly, but she liked dressing in short sexy clothes. He didn't mind if she dressed that way at home, but he thought her dressing sexy was inappropriate for church. He would talk to her about that, but she got upset and complained that he was being too controlling.

HELPING THE RELATIVES

A few years ago, Abby told Raymond that she wanted one of her brothers, a sister, and a nephew to come from their home country to live in America. They had never been to America and had no one else to help them. Abby begged Raymond to help. He loved his wife so he thought he should help her family.

Since her relatives didn't have money to come to America, Raymond and his parents showed evidence of support that was required by Immigration. A month later, he took out a loan at work to pay off her school fees.

When they lost the house in New Jersey to foreclosure, they moved into an apartment in Queens, New York City.

By this time, Abby's relatives got their visas. However, the three relatives did not have money to buy the three airline tickets. Meanwhile, Abby went back home to visit the relatives, but Raymond did not go. While there, she contacted Raymond and begged him to get a loan in order to buy the three airline tickets. He loved his wife, so he took out loans and bought the tickets that cost thousands of dollars.

As soon as the three relatives got to America, Raymond saw changes in Abby. Whenever he tried to talk to her, he felt she did not want to communicate with him. What he discussed with her, she would go and tell her relatives. He thought that was no good. He told her, "Let them go. Let them find their own place."

She said, "No, I don't want them to go."

He said, "No, that's not right."

He found Abby's three relatives now in the apartment which included Abby, their three children, her mother, and himself. That was nine people in their apartment. In fact, her mother had been living with them ever since they had gotten married.

The mother added to the confusion because she didn't want the three relatives to leave either. Abby said that the three relatives would help pay for the rent, but Raymond kept saying no. There were reasons he said no: (1) they had too many people living in that apartment; (2) it was against the law to have so many people in the apartment; (3) it would make a problem with the landlord; and (4) Abby and Raymond had no privacy.

Abby wanted them to buy a house that would give them more room and they could all live together. What bothered Raymond was that she still had relatives back in Africa who wanted to come to the U.S. The plan was that everyone could live in a house. Raymond said, "Your brother, sister, and nephew are here and they need to go look for their own place. We should be using our money to take care of our kids."

As anyone can understand, more relatives meant more stress. He was not a millionaire. He wondered how fast the relatives would find work. Even if they bought a house, he didn't like the idea of having four to ten relatives walking around in the house which meant giving up their privacy.

Abby said, "Okay, I'm going to speak to them." She spoke to them. She came back and explained to Raymond that her brother did not want to move in with his sister because the sister had not finished school. If he moved in with her, he was afraid the sister would not find a job and he would end up paying all the bills. Raymond said, "What are you talking about? Why am I different? If he does not want to move in with his sister, why would I want to stay with them and pay all their bills?"

The idea of relatives living with them created a big argument. In frustration, Raymond finally said, "No, I am not going to buy a house and fill it with relatives."

That's when she dropped the bomb and said, "If you cannot live with them, then I cannot live with you either. I don't love you anymore. I didn't know how to tell. I don't have feelings for you anymore." She also said that Raymond could live with her as a roommate, but they would not live as a husband and wife.

Raymond thought she was kidding. After she came back from Africa, everything started changing. She said to him that, if he wanted, he could stay with them and take care of the children. Meanwhile, a lot of money was being deducted to pay the loans he had taken out to help her relatives, but she didn't care. When she said she wanted a divorce, Raymond decided to move out. He wasn't ready to live with his wife as a roommate. The idea of giving up his wife was a tough decision for him to make.

Abby didn't want him to leave until he gave her the car keys. He wasn't ready to give her the car. She called the police and said he was going to kill himself. She wanted the police to come and have them get the car keys.

When the police came, Abby told them that Raymond was

going to take poison and that he had written a suicide note. He didn't know it, but she had hidden poison in the bathroom. She brought it out to show the police officers. The police asked Abby for the note that he wrote, but she couldn't find it. That was a lie because there was no suicide note. After all that drama, Raymond saw how devious she could be and decided he's getting out. The police saw through her scheme and told Raymond to sleep somewhere else that night. They didn't have a reason to arrest him, so he was free to go. Abby had also called Raymond's dad before the police came. When the police had arrived, Raymond's dad arrived too, so Raymond was ready to leave with him.

Instead of trying to drive away with the car, Raymond kept the keys and left with his dad in his car. About three hours later, Raymond came back for the car. He got in his car and drove it to his parents' home where he went back to bed. A few days later, Raymond drove back to give the car to Abby to use for the kids, but she refused it.

Raymond stayed with his parents for a couple of weeks. Because so many deductions were being taken out of his paychecks for loans to help her family, he didn't even have enough money to rent an apartment. With the help of a friend, he ended up renting a small room away from all the madness coming at him. After that night, Raymond was willing to forgive and forget for the sake of the children and remain married. He got on his knees and begged Abby to reunite for the sake of the kids, but she pushed him away. She said no.

Raymond then told the church elders and asked them to intervene with her. They went to their apartment to talk to her. She told them firmly that no, nothing could change her mind. She didn't want him anymore. Raymond asked the pastor and the pastor's wife as well as church members to talk to her, but she said the same to them. Since Raymond had moved out, she didn't want him back. Raymond felt that she did not care about the children. To him, he thought she was more concerned about her extended relatives and herself, with no concern for the children.

Meanwhile, Abby had been working. Fortunately, Raymond had finished paying for her education. He wanted to help her to finish school so she could get a steady job. For the sake of their children, he wanted them to save money for their education and not have to take out loans for their college education. However, he felt betrayed. It seemed that she was thinking differently; she had plans to leave him and live with her family.

Her brother and sister did get jobs, and the nephew went to high school since he could not work.

The first time Raymond told the pastor about the separation, the pastor was away at a convention, so he called him on the phone. That night Raymond cried as they talked on the phone and the pastor prayed with Raymond. The next day, the pastor called and prayed with Raymond again. When the pastor came home from the trip, he sat down with Abby and her relatives to discuss what could be done. After the pastor and elders visited Abby and her relatives, they did not come by to pray with Raymond. He had no idea why they didn't help him when he needed them the most.

For a few months, Abby stopped going to their church. He left her now in God's hands.

CHAPTER 38

MARRIAGE CONSIDERATIONS

Wisdom today: After the shock of facing a divorce, trust in another partner can be a difficult thing to regain in a second marriage.

The papers were done, and Raymond and Abby were divorced. They had joint custody of their children, so he would pick them up on the weekends. To him, being a good father meant always making sure the kids were okay.

Raymond was confused why Abby went to the extreme of calling in the police and then producing medications supposedly to prove that he was going to kill himself by overdosing. None of that was true. She created too much unnecessary drama. While married, he had Abby listed on his work insurance. As of now, he took her name off everything that he had. There have been so many crime stories on TV every week about husbands or wives who wanted to kill their spouses, usually to collect insurance money. It could be called death-by-spouse, but commonly involves a hit man or a hired killer.

DIVORCE NOT EASY IN GHANA

In Ghana, there are two ways to get married: (1) in the court with the lawyers and (2) traditional marriage by the elders. If a man wants to marry a girl, he would go to her family and request she leave them to be his wife. The man would have to prove he is ready to marry by showing that he has money, clothes, and wine. At the ceremony, everybody who comes is a witness.

If a spouse wants a divorce, the family of the spouse asking for the divorce has to bring back what was given; they have to repay the gifts. No matter how much time has passed.

These days there are more divorces than before. People customarily stayed together until one of them passed. They used to marry with love. If a person went back to the family, the family preferred to force the person back into the relationship.

In the past, the husband used to live in a separate place from the wife. The woman would cook and clean in her place. Then, she would bring food to the man at his place and stay the night with him. The next morning she went back to her mother, brothers, and sisters. At that time in the villages, this was considered a traditional marriage. In the cities, the married couple preferred living together.

Ghana has had a bad reputation of abusing widows. There is the case of a married man and woman who made enough money to buy three trucks for their farm and live in a house. When the husband died, the husband's family members claimed their inheritance rights to confiscate everything, including putting the woman out of the house. Widows had little or no rights. Some widows would resort to going to the local voodoo priest to get revenge against such cruel families. Putting widows on the street happens a lot. Christians are doing this too. How can anyone claim to be a Christian if they are hurting the widows? People need to practice their Christian conscience let alone their moral conscience. Not only is widow abuse hypocrisy, but it goes against the Bible's teaching to care for the poor. Also, Ghanaian widows usually don't have enough money to fight for their rights, while in the U.S. the widow would file a lawsuit to protect herself.

When a husband died, the husband's family used to be allowed to take everything away from the wife. It was never a nice practice and only placed more hardships on a widow who had no support. Still today, bad families will try to take everything away from the widow. The government has changed the law so that a wife is part of her husband's estate. This protects the widow, but it's hard to change old customs.

When Raymond and Abby divorced, she asked for two properties they owned in the home country. Instead of having any problems with her, he agreed to let her have the properties. He had no interest in contesting the properties.

If a Ghanaian spouse wants to get a divorce, the spouse can hire a lawyer or just go to the court to make the request without a lawyer. A copy of the divorce goes to both spouses.

It seems some people seek a divorce after coming to America because of what can be called the "dollar power." In most cases, the wife gets child support, which in effect can be like a job.

There have been cases where a spouse has enough money to secretly build a house in their home countries and live a double life—one life in their country and another with the spouse in America. Of course, not every man or woman is that devious.

ASK FOR A SECOND OPINION

Second opinions are common when facing a serious medical diagnosis and treatment. Second opinions about marrying someone could be the solution to help solve the high divorce rate in America. Maybe others can see things and offer honest opinions as to why someone should or should not marry that special someone. If someone is in love, it is normal to feel happy and to overlook the faults of the other person. That can prove to be a disaster later. Listen to the advice of others about marrying someone.

Rethink what could go wrong. Ask a lot of questions in order to save heartache and financial problems later. What would happen if things go wrong? Will the relationship always be a love relationship?

What other intentions do both parties have? Are there personality conflicts? Is there one dominant, controlling person or is it a balanced, diplomatic acceptance of each other? What about the future? How honest will both parties be with each other? Do both parties communicate openly or does someone hold secrets? Are the relatives too interfering? Is the partner interested in children's needs or only in what they want?

There is no way to tell which spouse will stay forever and which one will turn out to be devious and want a divorce. Devious people can be hard to spot before the marriage, but they have no qualms about bringing heartaches and troubles.

CHAPTER 39

SINGLE FATHER LIFE

Wisdom today: Raymond has learned to live a simple life: go to work, go to church, and stay at home after work. Other divorcees may like to run wild to date new people, but he feels he needs to reorganize his life and emotions.

WEEKENDS WITH THE KIDS

Raymond and his kids are very close. He picks them up some weekends, takes them to church, unless Abby brings them to church, and they sleep over at his place. On Sundays, he takes them out to run track, play soccer, or go for a walk in a local park when the weather permits. Since he had to move, he lives in a different community about 45 minutes away from his kids. He misses the little things he used to do every night with the kids. Even though he doesn't see them every day, he wants them to know he still loves them very much.

Raymond tells the kids, "We don't have a choice. Mother wants to live her life, so we have to move on with our lives in order to survive. We cannot live in the past or think about what has happened. There is an African saying: when two elephants fight, the grass suffers."

FATHER RESPONSIBILITIES

Raymond always made sure the children had a home and would not go homeless. He currently lives in one room, so there is no room for them to stay with him except for a weekend. It's best that they live with Abby where there is room, their grandmother can watch them, and they can attend their same schools. Raymond tries to keep things as normal as possible.

He and Abby only communicate about the kids. In fact, she told him not to call her, unless it has to do with the kids. That's what he does. Their only communication is about the children. That's fair with him because he does not want any unnecessary drama from Abby. In fact, Raymond doesn't know how she is doing with work and doesn't ask. Generally, what Abby has requested he has given her, except the car keys. Raymond prefers to cooperate and have a peaceful atmosphere for the kids. His motto is: I don't want to fight. I just want to move on with my life—and help the kids.

Raymond sees the children on the weekends and can call them anytime. They show him their school grades. They're all doing well in school. He missed the last parent-teacher conference meeting, but is determined to be at the next one. A teacher called to say the oldest boy was having a problem misbehaving in school. Abby went to the meeting, but Raymond didn't get there. He wasn't sure if the divorce caused his son to do something wrong or something else caused the problem. He and Abby had a meeting with the school's principal and some teachers to figure out what caused the problem and what to do. The meeting was successful with Raymond and Abby agreeing that the boy would meet with a counselor.

Raymond calls his son on the phone regularly during the week to encourage him to be good. On the weekends, he speaks with him about what is right and wrong, as well as about staying on the right track because his younger siblings are looking up to him as their role model.

When Raymond takes his children to church, they attend church school classes in addition to the church worship. Raymond is encouraged that the children are learning about God, morality, and living a righteous life. As parents, Abby and Raymond watch over their children in order to raise them to be prepared to be righteous adults.

As a single father, Raymond has the challenge of not being with his children enough. He believes he should be with the children in order to discipline them and, yet, they do need to obey their mother too. As for spending time with the kids and taking them places, he has no idea what their mother does for them.

If Africa, it's true that, if a child is insulting an adult or misbehaving, the adult can punish the child. In America, we can't be abusive or the family gets in trouble. In America, families have to follow American laws. Someone could get in trouble with the police if the children say in school that they were mistreated at home. The children can be taken away to a foster family. Since Raymond cannot accommodate having the children live with him, he emphasizes to Abby that everyone in the apartment has to treat the children the right way to avoid an investigation by the children's protective services.

According to the family judge, the children can live with either parent. Raymond cannot have the kids living with him seven days a week because he is not home when the children come home from school. An adult needs to be there. That presents a problem because Raymond does get home until around 8 p.m.

Their older son has started a new junior high school, so he takes a bus to school on his own. His younger children walk to the nearby elementary school with the help of their grandmother who can also meet them after school and walk them home. When Raymond and Abby were married, he used to drive the kids to school and go on to work.

The children and Raymond have a good time on the weekends when he is able to see them. They are always glad to see him and look forward to being with him every weekend. If he has chores and shopping to do on the weekends, he takes the children with him. They cooperate and help him out. They're good kids. Even though he's not there five days a week, he is still trying to keep them on the same right path so they will not change. They have a good foundation—the church and their public schools. Raymond still teaches them that good friends lead them the right way and bad friends lead them the wrong way. He constantly teaches them the importance of having good friends because they can do more in life with good friends.

CHAPTER 40

LIVING ALONE

Wisdom today: Children are constantly pressured to follow the crowd, but children can be a blessing when they follow adult the advice to be good and to do good to others.

In the beginning of the divorce, Raymond was in shock. Life was not easy. Abby seemed to be in her own world and not really caring about the kids. He could only wonder why she did what she did. He felt she used him rather than help him.

Raymond had no reason to visit her apartment. He was not welcome there, except to pick up the kids. Abby had told him that she wanted to explore life. She was about 24 when they married so she could not be considered a young teenager.

After Raymond went through a crying period, he finally decided that he would not let her kill the dreams he and the kids wanted. Now on his own, he doesn't count on Abby having enough money to pay for the college education of their children. He realizes he may have to help pay for their education as best as he can himself. He did not have education opportunities back home in Ghana, so he is determined that his kids will have opportunities for their education in America.

THE CHILDREN AND AFRICA

Raymond has told the kids stories and the history of Africa. It's hard for him to agree to allow the children to travel to Africa because he doesn't trust Abby or something bad might happen to them there. He feels he has to protect his kids by not letting them go out of the country until they are older.

Since the divorce, the kids can get a passport or visa, but it requires the consent of both parents. Raymond says no because he doesn't see any reason for the kids to go to Africa while they focus on their American education and he doesn't want Abby making surprise trips out of the country with the kids.

Raymond and Abby have taught the kids to speak their native African language at home, so they will be able to communicate with relatives in the native language when it's time for them to visit.

RAYMOND'S DEPRESSION

The kids are too young to make choices for themselves. That's why he has to live for them. Before he left, he told them in front of Abby why he had to leave, "Your momma said she doesn't want me anymore. She doesn't love me anymore and she didn't know how to tell me. She said she doesn't have feelings for me anymore if I don't go and buy a house with her and her extended family. She told me that she was going to explore life. She said we could live together like friends, but I told her I could not do that."

The children started crying. They made Raymond cry too. Their daughter told her mother, "I will never forgive you for this."

After Raymond left, everything was quiet. He came back to an empty apartment. There were no excited kids running around and telling him their stories. He went into a depression. He lost weight to the point that his parents worried about his health and they took him to the emergency room. He felt he was paralyzed. People shared their advice that helped. In addition, he kept reading his bible and praying. The divorce seemed to him to be his fault, making him feel ashamed and embarrassed. He tried to understand what he did wrong to have this happen. After a lot of thinking and praying, he realized that there were pressures on Abby from her family. It became a contest of wills between two families and different parties living in a cramped apartment.

It then dawned on him that he made a mistake by bringing her extended family to live with them. He thinks she listened to them and started making plans about what they wanted and not what they should be planning as a husband and wife. Without Abby's extended family influencing her thoughts, Raymond thinks they could still be happy together and saving money for the children's education.

Raymond doesn't know if Abby's extended family was more important to her than their own family and the kids' future. When Raymond married Abby, he considered her family his and his family hers, but then he saw changes as her family tried to take control of his family and tell him what to do.

RAYMOND'S NEW GOALS

Right now, Raymond's goal is to just live his life. He's afraid of getting involved with anybody else because he doesn't know what another woman might do to him. It may take years before he can trust another woman. He had put his whole heart into forming a relationship with Abby and having a family.

The best thing for him is to stay focused on his kids. With three kids, that's enough to keep him busy. He continues teaching the kids that they cannot do anything without God. In Proverbs 9:10, everyone is reminded that the fear of the Lord is the beginning of wisdom. He wants the kids to learn that wisdom and to live their lives based on that wisdom. If they don't have a healthy God-fearing respect for the Creator, they could grow up thinking they are more important than God and that would lead to their downfall.

The kids are pretty happy now. He wants them to stay happy because happiness can keep people healthy and get them through difficult times that will come to everyone. No one is immune from difficulties. When he picks up the kids, they're happy to see him. That's important that they have a great father-son and father-daughter relationship. Also, their happiness makes him happy. Depending on his job duties, the kids may not be able to see him on the weekends. They have to adjust to his being away at times.

Raymond knows that some Black men have had a notorious reputation for having children and then running away from their responsibilities as fathers. It is a sad comment when fathers do that. It has always been important to Raymond that his children know that he is not running away from them. He had to leave rather than cave in to the pressures of everyone at home telling him what to do and the humiliating fact that no one accepted what he wanted for the family. Too many pressures were placed on him. He was not going to do the bidding of what Abby and her relatives wanted. A man has to be a man in his own family or else he will feel that he is being taken advantage of.

The kids are respectful of others, especially adults, and he wants them to grow up to continue being respectful to everyone. He and Abby taught them from the beginning to show respect. God helped them to teach that lesson to the children. The children don't have a problem with respect. It's the same respect that Raymond was taught back home in Africa. He was taught to show respect by giving up his seat for a female to sit, Children were taught give their seats to adults and shake hands when someone says hello.

Raymond always prays to God that his kids will make the right choices. Choosing a friend is very, very important in life. Besides choosing a good school, choosing good friends can be life changing. Friends can determine our future. Friends can teach their friends to be honest or dishonest, to use drugs or not to.

Raymond's children tell him they are taking on responsibilities like getting themselves dressed for church. He used to help them dress when they were young, but now they get themselves ready. He has asked the elder son to help dress the young ones. He's happy to see the kids take on new goals of helping each other too. They are always a family and have to learn to help each other.

THE MOST DIFFICULT TIME IN HIS LIFE

Every relationship has problems. Learning that we must cope with problems is another reason for writing this book. Individuals and couples need to communicate with those who can help them analyze their problems. Couples need to solve their problems by mutual compromise and agreement. A spouse does not always get his or her way all the time. Raymond loved his family dearly, so it was hard to pack up his things and leave, He made the effort to talk to people in the church in order to rescue the marriage. The church pastor and elders did their part. Leaving his family was the most difficult time in his life.

A friend of Raymond's who worshiped at a different church on Sundays had her husband pray with Raymond many times. That helped him the most. Those who are willing to keep praying for him show that they are on his side and want the best for him.

Raymond doesn't know what Abby has said about him, but he has learned not to worry about that. The way he lives is an open book, and being open with others. God knows the truth and that's what counts to him. He can't dwell on the past. He goes to church to worship God. He knows the God he is worshipping. Afterwards, he is content just to come home.

This section ends Raymond's and Abby's story thus far, but it does not represent the end of their lives.

CHAPTER 41

RETIRE TO GHANA?

Wisdom today: I believe many more Americans have been retiring to Ghana nowadays because their U.S. dollars can get two to three times the buying power there and the friendliness of the Ghanaian people makes foreigners welcomed.

MY RETIREMENT?

People are building homes in Ghana for retirement and the country is much better than it used to be. Since Samuel Kwarteng's children are U.S. citizens and will probably establish their lives in the States, he doesn't expect to retire to Ghana. He expects to spend most of his retirement in the States with the children. His children should get their college degrees in the States and then it's up to them to find good jobs and have a better life. Their lives and careers in America should be blessed by God and be much different than what Samuel had experienced growing up in Africa.

GHANA THEN TO NOW

Is Ghana a safe place for retirement? There have been a growing number of articles about people from America and Europe retiring in African countries, including Ghana, because their money goes further and they can afford to enjoy retirement better in Africa.

Precautions are always necessary when retiring to another country. The following list highlights what a retiree needs to do:

1...**Escape money**. Have enough money to travel back to their country. If any (African) country erupts into violence or infrastructure services are not provided, a person may have to move away to a better country. An example of a country getting worse is Venezuela.

2...**Medical Emergencies**. Consider your medical needs. We've already discussed the limitations of ambulances and hospitals unless a person can afford care in a city hospital. There is quality medical care in many African countries and some hospitals are equipped to do sophisticated medical research. Some medical care is accessible, but with delays.

3...**Crime**. As we already discussed, tall walls, electronic security systems, good common sense, and a good rapport with the police will all offer a retiree better protection. There are criminals everywhere who try to take advantage of retirees, resulting in scams, robberies, and murder.

4...**Internal Travel**. Travel within any country can be dangerous. Not only may the roads be impassable and dangerous, but thieves and gangs will stop people at gunpoint to rob them or carjack their vehicles.

5...**Infrastructure**. How reliable are the infrastructures? Will a retiree have to have his own generator, well, or sewage system? What is provided reliably every day in developed countries may be interrupted every day or for weeks.

6...**Political Stability**. Consider how the political parties get along now and in the future. Is there freedom for opposition parties or is the president drifting towards becoming a dictator? Political corruption happens everywhere and it does not help the citizens. If the political parties do not cooperate and do nothing, there can be no improvements in the country; it will become known as a do-nothing country. Retirees should stay alert to citizen complaints; those complaints can lead to riots and political upheavals. Ghana is considered a stable country because it has held elections and opposing political parties have had a turn taking control of the government without bloodshed or a civil war. When civil war breaks out or a guerrilla force tries to take control of any government, the retirees need to have the money to move to safer countries. Bloodshed, civil wars, guerrillas, and terrorists can destabilize any government and cause its collapse. Retirees may enjoy retiring in luxury, but a country in turmoil is not safe. No one needs to stay in a collapsing country where the escape routes, including the airports, are shut down.

7...**Natural disasters**. Retirees can make their retirement dollars stretch very far and live like royalty in very poor countries, such as Nepal, but the recent earthquakes have proven that living in foreign countries may mean lack of medical help, food, and shelter when disasters occur.

8...**Personal rights**. A retiree has to ask a lot of questions and communicate with fellow countrymen already retired in Ghana or any country whether happiness can be found in the other country. One important question for Americans and others from democratic countries is do they lose their freedom?

If someone asked, is Ghana a good country where I could retire? The general answer would be yes. Ghana represents one of the better African countries. It would behoove any retiree to spend time in Ghana to evaluate whether there would be too much of a cultural shock to live there and whether the country offers enough outstanding benefits to justify spending a lot of years there.

Photo credit: Rita Gyamfuah
Figure 35   Sample Living Room

Photo credit: Rita Gyamfuah
Figure 36   Manet - Paradise Style Home

CHAPTER 42

GHANA TODAY

Wisdom today: Ghana can be considered an open society that has been making improvements in the last twenty years, but it needs faster improvements for everyone—citizens, tourists, politicians, and investors.

This chapter offers some last thoughts about Ghana. These are random ideas, but Ghana is on the verge of being a greater country.

FAST FOOD – POOR HEALTH

Most people are too poor to eat at a fast food restaurant, so those restaurants are limited to a few large cities. For the most part, Ghanaians in the villages and towns still prefer eating at home or from local food vendors. Their favorite foods include spinach, dried fish, palm soup, banku and okra soup, fufu and peanut soup on top, and tuosafe (a platter made with rice and, sometimes, meat). Water is the main drink of choice.

In the cities, Ghanaians are rejecting their culture and normal diets by switching to fast foods and sodas. Ghanaians now eat the French fries, pizza, and donuts imported from the American franchised restaurants such as Dunkin' Donuts and McDonald's. That food and the sodas at those restaurants have proven to cause obesity. Mayor Bloomberg of New York City saw the dangers of supersized sodas and tried to limit the sizes to help prevent obesity. Americans have been known to eat their way to obesity, diabetes, and poor health. It appears that Ghanaians will start a host of health problems the more they indulge in the American-style fast foods and sodas.

COMPUTERS FOR STUDENTS

In Ghana, the children and the schools don't have computers. Computers are necessary to advance any country. The Ghanaian government needs to collaborate with NGOs (Non-government agencies) to get computers into every classroom and given to every student. Obtaining computers is one of the greatest challenges facing the underdeveloped countries. This book asks these challenging questions: how many computers has the government placed in schools in Ghana? Can the government verify what it has done for the students? Are there multiple NGOs that can bring in several thousand computers for the Ghanaian students in order to help them to catch up with students in developed countries?

CAFES AND COMPUTERS – A RECENT CHANGE IN 10 YEARS

Today, Ghanaians listen to radios, watch the American TV shows such as *America's Got Talent*, and have internet connections to Google, Facebook, and cable TV. There are more Wi-Fi cafés in the cities where people can connect to the internet. Since laptops are very portable, relatives overseas will ship a computer, have a friend carry one in, or bring one themselves. Chinese-made computers are also sold in Ghana, but the Ghanaians complain that they break too easily. In Ghana, there are no inspections, so imported products tend to break down and there are most likely no product guarantees. People are allowed to sell whatever they want at the markets or stores without the government interfering or inspecting the quality of the products. In Ghana, everyone has to follow the old adage: buyer beware. There are no quality control checks, no guarantees, and no getting money back if something breaks.

SINGERS – NATURAL TALENT

In Ghana, there are not enough resources to teach students music or to buy them musical instruments. For centuries, people learn music however they can, make musical instruments, and develop their own musical styles. Women singers have grown in popularity in Ghana and Africa, just as they have in the U.S. Since most Ghanaian singers start by singing gospel, every church has its own star soloist or singing group. Today, it's very common for people to enjoy plenty of CDs, DVDs, and music videos from around the world. Small music studios have popped up throughout Ghana, helping to turn local musicians into celebrities. The Ghanaian music studios may not have the same sophistication as the U.S. studios, but local Ghanaian musicians now have opportunities for establishing a worldwide fan base.

CARS AND THE GOVERNMENT

Ghanaians have to import cars they buy. However, the government duty fees are often too much, so few people are able to buy cars. If duty fees were lower, people with jobs could afford the cars. Having cars in a country creates auxiliary jobs, such as taxis, gas stations, and auto mechanics.

The government does not want cars imported that are 10 years or older. Some people buy cars from Korea or Italy, but those cars have a bad reputation of catching fire and not lasting. There are no auto recalls. The government does not require the car manufacturers to fix any cars with manufacturing problems. Autos recalled in the U.S. will not be recalled in Ghana. People just keep driving their cars, no matter how bad the mechanical or pollution problems. Government-mandated inspection of cars and trucks would be a great step forward for protecting the people. There would be two significant results: (1) there would be jobs for auto inspectors and (2) safer cars would reduce the number of accidents caused by mechanical problems. Driver education classes taught in the cars and in classes would be good sources of income for the government. The benefits would be jobs for driving instructors and, again, in the reduction of accidents when people drive safely.

GHANAIAN MOVIES – GROWING INDUSTRY

Movies produced in Ghana fall under the general category of "African movies." Although there are not big-budget movies, there are some African actor superstars who team up with producers to make local movies. In Ghana, producers prefer to make movies based on true stories, which are designed to be educational; documentaries are very popular and produced more often, depicting life in Ghana; historical events in Ghana; and Christian miracles. Movie languages vary—some are only English; others are in local languages because the actors only know their local language; and some movies combine the languages.

In New York City, vendors and stores sell a lot of Ghanaian-produced movies, catering to the African population, while new movies are always becoming available on the internet and YouTube. In Ghana, the cities have movie theaters, but none are in the villages.

The movie industry does offer awards for the better movies. In 2014, it's interesting to note that India's film industry brought its awards ceremony to Tampa, Florida where the superstars and producers walked the green carpet, a takeoff on Hollywood's red carpet for the Oscars. While Hollywood represents the American film industry, India's film industry is called Bollywood and African film awards are called Nollywood. The N for Nollywood probably comes from the fact that producers from Ghana and Nigeria are collaborating on filmmaking. All African countries are making more local films and some are collaborating. In Africa, producers probably get back their production costs through promoting sponsors who support showing the movies.

CHRISTIAN CALENDAR

Since America and Britain sent missionaries to Africa, the Christians in Africa follow the same Christian calendar and similar traditions, such as sunrise services for Easter.

SOMETHING NEW - SPECIAL DAYS

Valentine's Day has come to Ghana. It was adopted from America as more Ghanaians embraced America's traditions. In addition, special days, such as Valentine's Day, are good days for helping businesses make money from buying flowers to eating out at restaurants.

Of course, every day should be a special day if two people love each other. Unfortunately, some husbands beat up and abuse their wives and then try to be nice one day a year. Abuse is not true love, but there are plenty of husbands (and probably some wives) in Ghana and every country that need to practice anger control and to stop abusing their loved ones.

SHOPPING IN GHANA

In Ghana, it's typical to shop in outdoor markets where people haggle over the final prices. Newcomers to Ghana who are buyers should never accept the vendor's first price. If a vendor does not negotiate, the buyer should feel free to go to another vendor.

Ghana is still mostly an agricultural society made up of small, family-run farms. Small businesses have been part of making America great, so plenty of Ghanaians would like to operate their own small business. The Ghanaian government should help people expand into small businesses that would provide for a growing economy and a tax based on small business growth.

SHOESHINE GROWNUPS

It's a shame when grownups still have to do shoe shining to help their families. It's a difficult job outside where temperatures climb to 100 degrees. Shoeshine people announce their availability by banging on their boxes to get attention. Some lucky boys meet rich men who hire them to work at their homes, may make them a business partner, or simply give them shelter.

There's the story of one orphan boy who worked shoe shining. He met a man who helped him out and then the man paid his airplane fare to start a new life overseas. The boy took the flight overseas. What happened after he got overseas is not known. Ghanaians always think life will be better overseas. They are industrious, hard workers, and willing to start at the bottom in order to get a chance. Besides, all Ghanaians feel a moral obligation to help their extended family. If they don't help, nobody else will.

FORCED OVERSEAS TO WORK

Many Ghanaians have traveled to Europe and England in search of work. For example, some Ghanaians go to Italy, learn Italian, and try to fit into Italy's society, while facing prejudice because of the thousands of illegal aliens coming into Europe in search of a safe place to live and work. Ghana is obligated to provide a better future for its people. Ghanaians, of course, would stay in their home country if they could find work, but desperation drives them to escape the poverty.

GARBAGE

In Ghana, people carry garbage on their heads to the dumpster, which can be about half a mile away or more. In the past, people used to dump the garbage in the bush. The government needs to design a better sanitation system for picking up garbage. Gas from rotting garbage in landfills may even be a source of fuel for the needed electricity. Proper sanitation programs would help keep the country clean and give sanitation jobs to more people.

FUNERALS

As part of the funeral customs in Ghana, the family members stay at home the first week when a family member dies. Then they bury the body. The funeral lasts two days. The Adventists hold funerals Thursdays and Fridays, and then have church on Saturdays where the members support the grieving family.

In Ghana, some families use a funeral as an excuse to spend money rebuilding their houses or to buy new clothes. They may want to send the dead person off with new things around them, while often neglecting the living. Those who spend money on the house or new clothes may not even be helping to educate their children. Another purpose for this book is to remind people to care for the living and not spend money on a dead relative.

Ghanaian widows are not supposed to do anything for 40 days. After the 40 days, the family decides if they kick the widow out. Some families don't even wait for 40 days, but kick the widow out right away. This is a strange custom and completely inhumane because the Bible teaches us to care for the widows.

There is the story of one widow who borrowed money from a friend for the funeral. People were supposed to give her contributions for the funeral expenses. Instead, the husband's family took the contribution money and didn't give her anything back. They took away all her belongings and kicked her out. She was lucky because she had children and they could take her in. If a widow has underage children, the widow may still be kicked out of the house and she cannot rely on children to help her. How many more widows have to suffer until Ghanaians start practicing compassion? Let's change what's wrong and join together to make a better society.

INFLATION

Ghana is run by U.S. dollars. In some hotels, travelers can only pay with dollars. Ghanaians are only paid in local money. When the dollar goes up, everything goes up. When the dollar drops, the prices in Ghana still stay the same, making it difficult for poor people buy things. Foreign residents can also be hurt by inflation because they have to pay more too.

IMPORTING A CAR

If you want to send a car back to Ghana, the import fees are based on the engine capacity. In addition, the officials can add more fees for various reasons. If the owner cannot afford to pay the fees, the government takes possession of the car. Of course, the officials always add on fees, such as parking lot fees to hold the car until it's picked up. The owner cannot negotiate to lower the fees. Importing a car is taking a chance because an owner could lose a car that would be worth thousands of dollars.

It should be mentioned that Togo, a neighboring African country, has a free port. It is time to compete. Why can't Ghana have a free port? Ghana claims to be richer than Togo based on Ghana's natural resources. This is another challenge to the government: allow a free port so more business can be directed to Ghana.

A DREAM COUNTRY SOME DAY?

Ghana has achieved a good reputation as a peaceful country among the African countries. People from other African countries have moved to Ghana and retirees have come in growing numbers in order to enjoy a peaceful, happier life with more spending power. Even though the Ghanaian government does not provide enough social services and infrastructure support as it should, the Ghanaians are recognized for being harmonious, friendly, and cooperative. If the government provided more and better services to the people, Ghana might become a dream country for people to live and retire happily.

INDEPENDENCE

Once Ghana lost its colony status with England and gained independence, Ghanaians have a new question: how fast can the wealth of the "Gold Coast" (Ghana's former name) be used to help the people? Are Ghanaians better off being independent? Of course, independence is always the better form of government and a democracy is always better than a dictatorship. Government is not about politicians getting big titles and secretly stealing money. The best governments are about how the politicians are helping the citizens, control the corruption, and making many new improvements all the time. Governments should be about the people.

Photo credit: Rita Gyamfuah
Figure 37   Sample Conference Room

Photo credit: Rita Gyamfuah
Figure 38   Manet Beach Resort

Appendix A
Interesting Facts About Ghana

Official website: **www.ghana.gov.gh**

1...**Center of the World**: (Wikipedia: Ghana) The Prime Meridian passes through Ghana, specifically through the industrial port town of Tema. Ghana is geographically closer to the **"centre" of the world** than any other country in the world; even though the notional centre, (0°, 0°) is located in the Atlantic Ocean approximately 614 km (382 mi) off the south-east coast of Ghana on the Gulf of Guinea.

2...**Largest Artificial Lake**: Lake Volta, the world's largest artificial lake

3...**Death Penalty**: Ghana exercises the death penalty for treason, corruption, robbery, piracy, drug trafficking, rape, and homicide.

4...**Money**: The economy of Ghana is tied to the Chinese Yuan Renminbi along with Ghana's vast gold reserves and in 2013 the Bank of Ghana (BoG) began circulating the Renminbi throughout Ghanaian state-owned banks and to the Ghana public as hard currency along with the national Ghana cedi for second national trade currency.

5...**Economic Progress**: The "Ghana Vision 2020" will see Ghana become the first country on the Africa continent to become a developed country from the years 2020 to 2029 followed by a newly industrialized country from the years 2030 to 2039 onwards

6...**Major Gold Producer**: Ghana is the designated 2nd largest producer of gold on the Africa continent behind the designated first South Africa.

7...**Nationalize**: The Parliament of Ghana has drawn plans to nationalize Ghana's entire mining industry for greater revenues for Ghana. Ghana is the designated 2nd largest producer of cocoa in the world, and other hydrocarbon exports such as crude oil and natural gas.

8...**Population**: Ghana's labor force in 2008 totaled 11.5 million Ghanaian citizens.

9...**Manmade Harbor**:
Tema harbor is Africa's largest manmade harbor.

10...**Crime:** Ghana is a key narcotics industry transshipment point and it is the largest transshipment point of narcotics industry on Earth.

11...**Languages:** The official language is English and is spoken by 90% of the inhabiting population; however, 75% of the inhabiting population also speak the Akan language, and 100% of the inhabiting population speak the Niger–Congo languages.

12...**Population:** Ghana had a 2010 reported inhabiting population of about 24 million inhabitants in which 15 million inhabitants were Ghanaian nationals with Ghanaian citizenship.

13... **Food:** Banku is a common Ghanaian starchy food made from ground corn (maize).

14...**Religions**: The majority of the population is Christian with Muslims the second largest.

15...**Capital**: Accra the largest city and the capital.

16...**Government:** Ghana is

a <u>unitary</u> <u>presidential</u> <u>constitutional</u> republic with
a <u>parliamentary</u> <u>multi-party system</u> and former alternating <u>military</u>
<u>occupation</u>. Following alternating military and civilian governments
in January 1993, the Ghana military government gave way to the
Fourth Republic of Ghana after presidential and parliamentary
elections in late 1992. The 1992 constitution divides powers among a
president, parliament, cabinet, council of state, and an independent
judiciary.

17...."Politics: Ghana is one of the more stable nations in the region,
with a good record of power changing hands peacefully." (BBC
News Africa – Ghana)

18...."Economy: Ghana is the world's second largest cocoa producer
behind Ivory Coast, and Africa's biggest gold miner after South
Africa. It is one of the continent's fastest growing economies, and
newest oil producer." (BBC News Africa – Ghana)

19...Democracy: "In April 1992 a constitution allowing for a multi-
party system was approved in a referendum, ushering in a period of
democracy." (BBC News Africa – Ghana) (Samuel age 16)

20...Model of Reforms: "A well-administered country by regional
standards, Ghana is often seen as a model for political and economic
reform in Africa." (BBC New Africa – Ghana)

21...Oil Discoveries:"The discovery of major offshore oil reserves
was announced in June 2007, encouraging expectations of a major
economic boost." (BBC News Africa – Ghana)

22...African Peacekeeper Role: "Ghana has a high-profile
peacekeeping role; troops have been deployed in Ivory Coast, Liberia,
Sierra Leone and DR Congo." (BBC News Africa – Ghana)

23...Yellow Fever Certificate Required: "A yellow fever health certificate is required by all to visit Ghana." (www.touringghana.com)

24…**Eco-friendly**: Ghana is an eco-friendly tourist country with a sunny equatorial climate.

25…**Government: Constitutional democracy**. Formerly a colony of Portuguese, English, Dutch, Swedes, and again the English, until the country gained independence on March 6, 1957. ??**July 1, 1960**.

26…**Problems Continue** (Africa and Ghana): poverty, unemployment, literacy, child mortality, female exploitation, traffic, unreliable water, frequent power outages, and no welfare state. (See artcle by Afua Hirsch, Ghanian returnee from England to Ghana: **http://www.theguardian.com/world/2012/aug/26/ghana-returnees-afua-hirsch-africa**).

27…**Flights to Accra** (Ghana's capital): Available through the major airlines—British Airways, Lufthansa, Delta and KLM Airways to Kotoka International Airport in Accra. **(http://www.economytravel.com/africa/airfare-to-ghana)**

28…**Child Labor and Slavery**: In some places, children are, sometimes, hired out as indentured servants. Described in a *New York Times* article. **(http://www.nytimes.com/2006/10/29/world/africa/29ghana. html?pagewanted=all&_r=0)**

29…**Slave Trading**: formerly practiced in Ghana and other West African countries. "The volume of the slave trade in West Africa grew rapidly from its inception around 1500 to its peak in the eighteenth century. Philip Curtin, a leading authority on the African slave trade, estimates that roughly 6.3 million slaves were shipped from West Africa to North America and South America, about 4.5 million of that number between 1701 and 1810. Perhaps 5,000 a year were shipped from the

Gold Coast alone. The demographic impact of the slave trade on West Africa was probably substantially greater than the number actually enslaved because a significant number of Africans perished during slaving raids or while in captivity awaiting transshipment. All nations with an interest in West Africa participated in the slave trade. Relations between the Europeans and the local populations were often strained, and distrust led to frequent clashes. Disease caused high losses among the Europeans engaged in the slave trade, but the profits realized from the trade continued to attract them." **(http://www.ghanaweb.com/GhanaHomePage/history/slave-trade.php)**

Appendix B
Interesting Websites About Ghana

1… **www.gadling.com/2012**
10 Reasons to Visit Ghana:
  1…Rich history
  2…Lively Drum and Music Culture
  3…Budget Friendly
  4…Volunteer Opportunities
  5…Friendly People
  6…Natural Experiences
  7…Beautiful Beaches
  8…Unique Foods
  9…Laid-back Villages
  10..Handicrafts and Art

2…**http://www.ghanacelebrities.com/2012/10/29/lifestyle-ten-most-beautiful-tourist-attraction-sites-to-visit-in-ghanawhere-have-you-been-before-where-would-you-l**
10 Places to Visit in Ghana

3…**http://www.tripadvisor.com/Tourism-g293796-Ghana-Vacations.html**
82 Things to Do in Ghana

4… **www.ghanaweb.com**
Comprehensive directory of 3,000 Ghana-related websites.
Includes a good list of FAQs (Frequently Asked Questions)
    "Ghana, a country on the West Coast of Africa, is one of the most thriving democracies on the continent. It has often been referred to as an "island of peace" in one of the most chaotic regions on earth. It shares boundaries with Togo to the east, la Cote d'Ivoire to the west, Burkina Faso to the north and the Gulf of Guinea, to the south. A recent <u>discovery of oil</u> in the Gulf of Guinea could make

Ghana an important oil producer and exporter in the next few years."

5... **www.cia.gov/library/publications/the-world-factbook/geos/gh.html**
Central Agency Intelligence (CIA) World Factbook

6... **http://www.bbc.co.uk/news/world-africa-13433790**
Country profiles and news.

7... **http://www.irinnews.org/country/gh/ghana**
Humanitarian news and analysis: a service of the UN Office for the Coordination of Humanitarian Affairs.

8...**www.touringghana.com**
Where to go, where to eat, where to stay, festivals, and a lot more.

9... **http://www.infoplease.com/country/ghana.html**
Facts and figures about Ghana.

10.. **www.worldatlas.com/webimage/countrys/africa/gh.htm**
Interesting maps and iformation about Ghana.

11..**www.theguardian.com/world/2012/aug/26/ghana-returnees-afua-hirsch-africa**
"There is plenty of poverty to be attracted to. Average life expectancy is still only 56 years, child mortality remains high at 127 per 1,000 live births in 2010, and overall literacy rates are only 67%. Africa's economic growth is often described as "jobless" for its failure to create jobs, in particular for the 60% of Africans aged between 15 and 24 who are unemployed and who, a recent report found, have given up on finding work.
With these seemingly incompatible realities existing side by side, there is increasingly a PR war for the image of Africa overseas.
The *Economist*, still apologizing for its "hopeless continent" issue in 2000, recently branded Africa "hopeful" instead. Most international

news outlets now have programs or seasons specifically designed to champion positive news stories in Africa. The BBC runs *African Dream*, a series about successful African entrepreneurs, while CNN has *African Voices*.

But it is not the role of the media to sell a rebranded version of Africa, any more than it was right to paint it as the heart of darkness in the past. The problems remain and they are real. Since I moved to Ghana in February as west Africa correspondent for the Guardian and Observer, there have been two military coups. Everyone living in Ghana – rich and poor – is lumped together in a permanent jumble of terrible traffic, unreliable water and frequent power outages. Poverty is real here, there is hunger and disease, and there is no welfare state. Far from setting out policies that promise any real social change, many African governments are focused instead on administering foreign aid and directing showcase infrastructure projects that do little to benefit ordinary people." (Afua Hirsch, journalist, article about returning to her ancestral homeland, Ghana)

12..
www.nytimes.com/2006/10/29/world/africa/29ghana.html?pagewanted=all&_r=0
Joao Silva for *The New York Times*
"Indentured children as young as 5 and 6 sustain the fishing trade in Kete Krachi, without schools or basic necessities.
Shivering in the predawn chill, he helped paddle a canoe a mile out from shore. For five more hours, as his coworkers yanked up a fishing net, inch by inch, Mark bailed water to keep the canoe from swamping.
He last ate the day before. His broken wooden paddle was so heavy he could barely lift it. But he raptly followed each command from Kwadwo Takyi, the powerfully built 31-year-old in the back of the canoe who freely deals out beatings.
"I don't like it here," he whispered, out of Mr. Takyi's earshot.

Mark Kwadwo is 6 years old. About 30 pounds, dressed in a pair of blue and red underpants and a Little Mermaid T-shirt, he looks more like an oversized toddler than a boat hand. He is too little to understand why he has wound up in this fishing village, a two-day trek from his home.

But the three older boys who work with him know why. Like Mark, they are indentured servants, leased by their parents to Mr. Takyi for as little as $20 a year.

Until their servitude ends in three or four years, they are as trapped as the fish in their nets, forced to work up to 14 hours a day, seven days a week, in a trade that even adult fishermen here call punishing and, at times, dangerous."

Appendix C
Interesting YouTube Sites About Ghana

"Ghana Couple Writes Book"
"Ghana Living"
"73 Dollars Per Month 2 Bedroom Apartment Live Abroad Retirement"
"Ghana Music"
"Ghana Gospel Music"
"Ghana High Life"
"Ghana Praise/Worship"
"Ghana"
"Ghana Women Scams"
"Romance Scams – The Faces Behind the Masquerade"
"How Not to Get Scammed by Ghana Internet Scams"
"Internet Scamming in Ghana"
"Beautiful Ghana Song"
"Beautiful Ghana Women"
"Ama Beautiful Ghana Movie"
"Beautiful Ghana" (beautiful places and song)
"My Beautiful Ghana"
"Beautiful Music of Ghana"
"Ghana Most Beautiful 2011's Project"
"Ghana Music & Images"
"Images of Ghana"
"Accra Greater Accra"
"Ghana Bungalow for Sale (Case Study)"
"A Day in the Life in Ghana"
"I Love My Life in Ghana!"
"Beautiful Homes in Ghana"
"Ghana Property Online"
"Real Estate and Lands for Sale in Accra Ghana"
"President Obama's Visit to Ghana"

Appendix D
Ghanaian Christian Folk Song

367   Jeṣu, Jeṣu, Fill Us with Your Love

CHEREPONI   Irregular with refrain

Ghanaian folk song
Trans. Tom Colvin, 1969

Ghanaian folk melody
Adapt. Tom Colvin, 1963
Arr. Jane Marshall, 1982

Je - su,   Je - su,   fill   us with Your love, Show

us how to serve   the   neigh-bors we have   from You.

1. Kneels at   the feet of   His   friends,   Si - lent - ly wash - es their
2. Neigh-bors are   rich   and   poor,   Var - ied in   col - or and
3. These are the   ones we should serve,   These are the ones we should

4. Lov - ing puts us   on our knees,   Serv - ing as though we are
5. Kneel at   the feet of our friends,   Si - lent - ly wash - ing their

feet,   Mas - ter who acts as a   slave   to   them.
race,   Neigh-bors are   near and far   a - way.
love.   All   are neigh-bors to   us   and You.

slaves,   This is the way we should live with You.
feet,   This is the way we should live with You.

Appendix E
Unfinished Projects in Ghana

Volunteer Building Projects in Ghana | Projects Abroad
www.projects-abroad.org › Projects › Volunteer Abroad › Building
Volunteer on a Building **Project in Ghana** with **Projects** Abroad
and help ... the rains come and wash any **unfinished** structures away,
but the **projects** would not ...

C TONGU: Assembly completes unfinished projects - Ghana ...
www.**ghana**districts.gov.gh/news/?read=49604&sports
The Central Tongu District Chief Executive (DCE), Alhaji Bubey
Dzinadu says the NDC government has left a legacy of continuity in
development **projects**, ...

Assembly lauded for executing more projects - Ghana ...
ghanadistricts.com/news/?read=46836
Ashanti; Brong Ahafo; Central; Eastern; Greater **Accra**; Northern;
Upper East ... however urged the assembly to step-up work to
complete **unfinished projects** in ...

Ghana News - Gov't hands over uncompleted affordable ...
myjoyonline.com/.../govt-hands-over-**unfinished**-affordable-
housing-**pr**...
Mar 25, 2014 - Government has officially handed over the
uncompleted affordable housing **projects** at Borteman to the Social
Security and National Insurance ...

As I Journey Along: A Ghanaian's Perception of Life in the ...
https://books.google.com/books?isbn=141165997X

Gabriel Awuah - 2005 - Travel
... go back to search for additional money for their **unfinished**
project. For some people, travelling down to **Ghana** often to
oversee their housing project would be ...

Unfinished building - Wikipedia, the free encyclopedia
https://en.wikipedia.org/wiki/**Unfinished**_building
Wikipedia

Many construction or engineering **projects** have remained **unfinished** at various stages of development. The work may be finished as a blueprint or whiteprint ...

Youth In Agriculture in Ghana Series Pt 1: Ruth | Unfinished ...
unfinishedstories.net/2015/.../youth-in-agriculture-in-**ghana**-series-pt-1-ruth...
Mar 30, 2015 - At **Ghana's** agricultural colleges, graduates used to be guaranteed jobs ... The **project** doesn't provide funding for the students' businesses in ...

Building Volunteering in Ghana - Projects Abroad
www.projects-abroad.co.uk › Volunteer Projects › Building
Join one of our voluntary Building **projects in Ghana**. ... reach completion before the rains come and wash any **unfinished** structures away, but the **projects** would ...

Gov't hands over unfinished affordable housing project to ...
www.modern**ghana**.com/.../govt-hands-over-**unfinish**...
ModernGhana.com
Mar 25, 2014 - Gov't hands over **unfinished** affordable housing **project** to SSNIT ... units, including Borteman Housing **Project**, in the Greater **Accra** region and ...

[PDF]A Model for Reactivating Abandoned Public Housing ...
- iiste
www.iiste.org/Journals/index.php/CER/article/viewFile/11697/12054
by K Twumasi-Ampofo - 2014 - Cited by 1 - Related articles
6. A Model for Reactivating Abandoned Public Housing Projects in. **Ghana**. Kwadwo ..... 2 New Government to Complete **Unfinished Projects**. It is very sad that it ...

Samuel Kwarteng

ABOUT THE AUTHORS

SAMUEL KWARTENG was born and raised in Ghana (West Africa). At age 19, he came to the United States along with his siblings to live with their parents in Queens, New York City. He went on to further his education in the U.S. and has made a career with the United States Postal Service in New York City. He is an active member of the Seventh Day Adventist Church and has four children. His goal is to help others through this inspirational book and with other projects that are in development.

DONALD MACLAREN, Master's Degree, has been a ghostwriter and screenwriter for U.S. and international clients. He has helped to write, edit, and publish more than 30 books and five screenplays. He continues to work as a ghostwriter and screenwriter for United States and international clients. He is available at his email: **worldconnectg@gmail.com** and his cell phone: **718-932-7720.**

Donald MacLaren

You can reach the authors for speaking engagements and for other questions:

Samuel Kwarteng   (347) 319-8595

kwartengs14@yahoo.com

Donald MacLaren   (718) 932-7720

worldconnectg@gmail.com